SCUBA DIVING

Underwater Adventuring

Sports Illustrated Winner's Circle Books

BOOKS ON TEAM SPORTS

Baseball
Football: Winning Defense
Football: Winning Offense
Hockey
Lacrosse
Pitching

BOOKS ON INDIVIDUAL SPORTS

Bowling
Competitive Swimming
Golf
Racquetball
Skiing
Tennis
Track: Championship Running

SPECIAL BOOKS

Canoeing
Fly Fishing
Scuba Diving
Strength Training

SCUBA DIVING

Underwater Adventuring

by Hank Ketels and Jack McDowell

Photography by Jack McDowell and Pete Nuding

Illustrations by Robert Handville

Sports Illustrated
Winner's Circle Books
New York

Adapted from a book originally published by Little, Brown and Company titled *Safe Skin and Scuba Diving*. Copyright © 1975 by Little, Brown and Company, Inc.

Photographs on pages 12, 70, 77, and 118: Jack McKenney
Photographs on pages 36, 82, and 92: Robert Evans
Photograph on page 173: ANIMALS ANIMALS/R.F. Head
Photograph on page 174: ANIMALS ANIMALS/Robert Redden
Photograph on page 176: ANIMALS ANIMALS/Tim Childs
Photograph on page 177: ANIMALS ANIMALS/Amil Myshin
Photograph on page 179: ANIMALS ANIMALS/Steve Earley

All other photographs by Jack McDowell and Pete Nuding

NAUI Dive Tables, page 207: courtesy, National Association of Underwater Instructors
NAUI Dive Planning & Recording Worksheet, page 208: courtesy, National Association of Underwater Instructors
DAN Form, page 204: courtesy Divers Alert Network
CPR in Basic Life Support, page 190: reproduced with permission.
  © *Cardiopulmonary Resuscitation*, American Heart Association

This book is intended as a supplement to professionally-sanctioned courses in scuba diving instruction. Before attempting any dive, you should seek out and pass the appropriate level course from a certified scuba diving instructor. You should also check with your health care practitioner to make sure it is appropriate for you to undertake scuba diving. Follow your instructor's teaching carefully, and be aware that attempting the techniques and using the equipment discussed in this book could result in death or physical injury for which the authors, Sports Illustrated Winner's Circle Books and Time, Inc. will not be responsible.

Library of Congress Cataloging-in-Publication Data

Ketels, Henry.
  Sports illustrated scuba diving.

  (Sports illustrated winner's circle books)
  "Adapted from . . . Safe skin and scuba diving"—T.p. verso.
  1. Scuba diving. I. McDowell, Jack. II. Handville, Robert. III. Sports illustrated (Time, inc.) IV. Ketels, Henry. Safe skin and scuba diving. V. Title. VI. Title: Scuba diving. VII. Series.
  GV840.S78K474 1988   797.2′3   87-32380
  ISBN 0-452-26108-2 (pbk.) 88 89 90 91 92 AG/HL 10 9 8 7 6 5 4 3 2 1

Contents

Appendixes

Preface

Each year new surveys point to freshening surges in the tremendous popularity of sport diving. Each year more men, women, and children are certified in schools, at dive shops, and through special courses and eagerly take to the water. What is it about the underwater world that captivates so many people, that entices them away from familiar surroundings into a totally different environment?

A good part of the adventure of diving is in the lure of the unknown; more lies in the promise of momentarily escaping from a sometimes too-familiar, too-crowded environment. On land we are pressed in by buildings, vehicles, people; underwater the space is open, seemingly boundless. On land our ears are filled with the clamor of engines, drills, hammers; underwater there is stillness broken only by the sound of our own breathing. For the greater part of our lives we remain in close contact with the earth, ever aware of the pull of gravity; underwater we are free to drift as lightly as a feather. Little wonder that people are desirous to enter that peaceful realm, to leave for even a short while the confinements of civilization. This book, then, has a two-fold purpose: to introduce you to some of the marvels of the world just below the surface and to help prepare you to enter and enjoy it safely.

ACKNOWLEDGMENTS

The authors wish to thank Jerry Ingersoll and his staff, of the Outrigger Dive Shop in Campbell, California, for the use of much of the equipment pictured herein. A tremendous debt of gratitude is owed the many teaching assistants

10 and students who, through suggestions, questions, and practical examples triggered inspiration for much of the material in this book.

Special thanks and appreciation go to Sandi Ketels for her encouragement and for the many hours she spent editing and finalizing the manuscript, and to Carole Peirce McDowell for providing valuable insights as well as constructive criticism.

Finally, thanks to Pete Nuding for the additional photography he provided for this new edition.

—Hank Ketels and Jack McDowell

SCUBA DIVING

Underwater Adventuring

Free! Unencumbered by hoses and helmets, a scuba diver
moves effortlessly in three dimensions.

1

From Out of the Past

A Review of Man's Exploits Underwater

Man's varied excursions and explorations underwater are nothing new in the stream of history. More than four hundred years before the birth of Christ, Xerxes I, the bold king of Persia, was said to have employed combat divers in his seagoing campaigns. The tables were turned on Xerxes, however, when his men took captive a Greek by the name of Scyllias of Scione and held him shipboard prisoner along with several of his countrymen. Learning of Persian plans for an attack on a Greek flotilla, Scyllias distinguished himself for all time by seizing a knife and leaping overboard. As his captors rushed to the ship's side, Scyllias took a deep breath and dived under the keel. There he remained until the excitement over his escape had died away and the Persians turned to preparations for the forthcoming battle. Scyllias returned to the surface cautiously and bided his time until dark. Once sure of being unobserved, he worked his way from ship to ship, cutting each loose from its moorings. Then he swam several miles through and under the drifting, colliding Persian fleet to rejoin the Greeks off Cape Artemisium.

Scyllias's achievement was but one of many described by the ancient writers, who de-

13

lighted in recording deeds of heroism and daring and who did not hold back from embroidering fact with bits of fiction for the sake of glorifying the incidents. Athenian underwater soldiers were instrumental in destroying enemy coastal defenses at Syracuse. Military divers hacked at ships' cables at Byzantium. After battles they salvaged sunken vessels. Between wars they dived for sponges and coral at depths of 75 to 100 feet on a single breath of air, sometimes dropping to the bottom by holding a large stone.

BARRELS, BLADDERS, AND BELLS

Many early attempts at staying underwater bordered on sheer fantasy and are remembered more for their inventive genius than for their success. Experimental outfits, such as a leather hood that covered a diver's head and connected to the surface with a leather tube, or a breathing bag made from a sheep's bladder and sealed with wax to contain air, were exotic and noble tries. Such refinements did allow men to swim beneath the surface, but they could go only a foot or two down because of the difficulty of inhaling and exhaling against increasing water pressure on air hoses and rib cages. Upright diving barrels with one open and one closed end were an early try at increasing the amount of available air, but even a captive bubble of air becomes stale and is displaced by water after a short time. A painting that appeared in a Hindustani manuscript around the late 1500s shows a calm Alexander the Great descending into the Mediterranean in a kind of barrel. The twenty or so onlookers and attendants appear much more concerned than the diver.

In the sixteenth century Greek adventurers devised a bell-like device that was supplied with air from the surface. Weighted, and lowered to just a few feet off the bottom, it allowed a diver to stand on the sea floor while breathing fresh air. It was a remarkable technical advancement that allowed divers to go deeper and spend more time below than was possible either on a single breath of air or in a one-ended cylinder.

Several forms of diving bells were used successfully in Spain, France, Scotland, and England during the 1600s and 1700s, chiefly for salvage work. Perhaps the most noteworthy operation was carried off in 1687 by William Phips, a resolute New Englander who recovered 1.5 million dollars' worth of silver and gold from a Spanish galleon that had gone down off the coast of Haiti. Phips used native divers, who worked from bells suspended just above the bottom. The favorable outcome of the venture infected a good part of Europe

An early "skin" diver breathes from a leather bag while strolling casually along the ocean bottom. He is apparently unaware that his breathing time is counted in seconds because after an exhalation or two the bag will contain carbon dioxide instead of air.

with fortune-hunter's fever, and the methods by which the hoard was removed stimulated further underwater experimentation. During the 1700s full diving suits of leather were used to depths of 60 feet in England and France, and helmeted outfits supplied with air pumped down from the surface were tested in France and Germany. C. H. Klingert, a German engineer, devised a suit rigged with a sort of bellows, and later he put on a flexible air tank that was compressed by water pressure. Klingert also tried out a tin helmet. This crude affair enjoyed only limited success, but it was a step beyond the barrels, leather tubes, and compressible bags that were then being used.

The centuries-old diving bell held air well enough to allow divers to remain underwater for relatively long periods, but their movements were confined to the immediate region of the container. They didn't have to go to the surface often, but having to return to the bell for every breath of air meant that they couldn't go very far. John Lethbridge, an English scientist, put thought to the matter, and in 1715 he devised a diving suit that was more a man-sized chamber than an article of wear. In a closed cylinder that was turned on its side, a diver lay on his stomach and shoved his arms through a pair of leather sleeves, viewing the sea floor and his work through a glass port. Air in the chamber was kept at atmospheric pressure by means of a surface hose. However, because water pressure on the occupant's arms was uncomfortable, dive depths and time were limited.

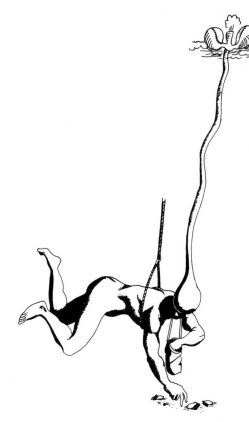

A long breathing tube leading to the surface works fine in theory but not in practice. At only a foot or so below the surface, water pressure would flatten the hose and compress the diver's chest so much that he wouldn't be able to draw a breath.

A leather hood and hose supposedly kept this salvage diver supplied with surface air, and the rope around his waist kept him from wandering too far. But with no weights to offset natural buoyancy, what kept him on the ocean bottom?

HELMETS, BREATHING BAGS, AND AIR TANKS

One of diving's most significant breakthroughs came in 1819 with the invention of a diving helmet. Augustus Siebe, a German artillery officer who emigrated to England after the Napoleonic wars, devised what was, in effect, a miniature diving bell with a window. It fitted over a man's head and was held on his shoulders with weights. Air was pumped to the helmet from the surface through a hose. Siebe's next step was to seal the helmet to a watertight rubber suit, which could be inflated to balance water pressure. This outfit was the prototype of subsequent helmeted suits, the so-called hard-hat rig in use today in many forms of salvage and prolonged underwater work. In 1825 another Englishman, W. H. James, demonstrated an underwater suit that had a self-contained air supply in the form of a small metal cylinder that attached directly to the diver. Since the tank's thin walls could not withstand much pressure, the invention didn't arouse much interest. But in 1865 two French inventors—Benoit Rouquayrol and Auguste Denayrouse—put a steel tank of compressed air on a diver's back, connecting it through a valve arrangement to a mouthpiece. Unlike a bell or a helmet, which supplies a constant flow of air, this arrangement gave air only when it was needed. The diver was not independent, though, because the tank had to be supplied with air through a hose connected to a pump at the surface.

The year 1869 saw publication of Jules Verne's book, *Twenty Thousand Leagues Under the Sea,* a fascinating novel whose oceangoing adventurers lived alternately on the sea floor and in a huge submarine that had all the comforts of home. The tale, which made reference to the Rouquayrol-Denayrouse apparatus, fired the creative imagination of generations to come. Whether inspiration was provided more by the fanciful Verne or by the practical scientists, the late 1800s witnessed much research and experimentation in submarines, especially in the United States, Russia, England, and France.

In 1911 Sir Robert Henry Davis, English chemist, physicist, and submarine engineer, developed an oxygen lung for the purpose of safely rescuing trapped crewmen from submarines that had gone to the bottom. The Davis submarine escape apparatus was a free-diving (no air hose to the surface), closed-circuit system. It consisted of a small tank of oxygen and a breathing bag containing caustic soda. The diver's exhalations passed through the chemical, which "scrubbed out" the carbon dioxide, returning pure oxygen to him. The Davis lung was used innumerable times throughout World War I to escape from wrecked submarines. (Although very dangerous below 25 feet, where pure

Alexander the Great, according to early writers, descended dry into the sea in a closed device that kept air in and water out. Sometimes pictured as an inverted cup, other times as a glass sphere, the diving chamber is here depicted as a transparent box housing a somewhat glum Alexander.

oxygen becomes poisonous to the human body, the lung had some limited military use in World War II because it gave off no telltale bubbles.)

In 1926 a French naval officer, Yves Le Prieur, modified the Rouquayrol-Denayrouse invention by ingeniously combining a specially designed demand valve with a high-pressure air tank to give a diver complete freedom from restricting hoses, entangling lines, and hazardous chemicals. Le Prieur's system was basically an air tank connected to a face mask, with a hand-operated valve that regulated the flow of air. The diver adjusted the amount of air he needed, depending on his depth, and the overflow escaped from around the edge of the mask. Whereas the Rouquayrol-Denayrouse tank held air at low pressure—less than 500 pounds per square inch—Le Prieur's cylinder withstood 1,500 pounds per square inch. Because the Le Prieur apparatus did not depend on a surface-connected air hose for breathable air, it is sometimes referred to as the earliest scuba (self-contained underwater breathing apparatus) system.

Although the major part of equipment research was being carried on in

France and other parts of Europe during the twenties and thirties, there was diving activity elsewhere, too. In Samoa, coral reef studies were being carried out by divers, and in the Galápagos and other parts of the Pacific, scientific dives were being made. In 1923 an oxygen rebreathing system, the Momsen lung, was adopted by the U.S. Navy for submarine escapes. In 1934 the first sport diving club, the Bottom Scratchers, was formed by a group of ardent California snorkelers and spear fishermen. Not to be outdone, the equally enthusiastic French founded their own amateur diving group, the Club des Sous-l'Eau. In 1938 a happy Anglo-Franco contribution appeared in the form of a book: *The Compleat Goggler.* The author was Guy Gilpatric, an American writer living in France, who divided his time between penning tales of Mr. Glencannon, a hard-drinking Scottish merchant seaman, and spearing fish underwater in the Mediterranean.

At the beginning of World War II sport divers were staying underwater only as long as a gulp of air allowed, since they had no breathing apparatus to extend their bottom time. Working divers still wore canvas suits, clumsy weighted shoes, and cumbersome copper helmets connected to the surface with lifelines and air hoses. Their alternative was an open-ended helmet that sat on the shoulders, but it, too, tied them to the surface with an air hose. Both rigs allowed good underwater time, but both were restrictive in that standing up-right was the rule. If a suited diver were to bend over too far, air would rush to the legs of his suit, inverting him and possibly ballooning him to the surface. An open helmet—still basically an inverted bucket kept empty of water by air pressure—that happened to be tilted too far would spill its air and fill with water, sending the diver to the surface too fast for his own good.

DIVING BENEFITS FROM THE WAR

The war years in France brought together Georges Comheines, Jacques Cousteau, and Émile Gagnan, a versatile trio whose combined efforts revolutionized the diving world. Frustrated by the occupation of their country, and bored for lack of something constructive to do with their time, the three daringly carried out a series of furtive experiments as a means of exploring the underwater world, knowing that if their equipment was discovered by the Germans, even though it was not meant as a military tool, it would be confiscated and they would perhaps lose their lives. By connecting a Rouquayrol-Denayrouse regulator to a Le Prieur high-pressure air tank, the inventor-explorers were able to dive to 174 feet, loosed from all surface hoses and lines. In 1943 Cousteau and

Gagnan made refinements in their exhaust system, perfecting a self-contained breathing unit that could be used underwater in any position. They named their invention the Aqua-Lung. In his early writings Cousteau lyrically described his incredible sense of freedom at being able to escape to another world, a world in which gravity was virtually nonexistent.

The war years in Italy were not lacking in underwater activity. The Davis oxygen lung was pressed into service against the British by a group of Italian underwater demolition workers. A few of the men were explosives experts; others were adventurers and patriots. Some were even able to swim. Two-man teams rode astride slow-moving, underwater electric torpedoes, many of which sank to the bottom long before they reached their destination. At Gibraltar, the surviving "pigs" or "chariots" were steered through protective nets and booms to the sides of Allied ships, where the underwater crews fastened timed explosives to the hulls. Many ships were thus decommissioned suddenly when their plates were blown in. The deeds of the Italian charioteers echoed the exploits of Xerxes' divers more than two thousand years earlier.

The diving bell, depicted here in a see-through version to show the worker within, was perhaps the most successful of all devices tried by early experimenters. In the eighteenth century a wooden bell was used by several divers for more than an hour, the air being replenished from barrels brought down from the surface.

Early in 1943 the United States organized its first combat swimmers in the Pacific theater of operation. Shaken by the tragic invasion of Tarawa, in which more than a thousand invading Marines were killed and twenty-five hundred wounded because they couldn't get over the island's reef, the Navy called for volunteer swimmers to clear invasion paths through shoal waters. Their purpose was straightforward; their job, extremely hazardous. The Underwater Demolition Team (UDT) was trained for close, prelanding reconnaissance of reefs and beaches—"close" meaning within arm's reach. The men were dropped from rubber boats to swim and wade inshore, where they planted and detonated underwater explosives to knock out natural and manmade obstacles. They mapped minefields laid by the enemy simply by swimming among the mines and counting them, then drawing charts on slates. Often they cut underwater cables so the mines would bob to the surface; sometimes they blew them up in place. The UDT did all this under fierce Japanese shore defenses while carrying explosive packs and wearing no more than sneakers, swim trunks, and face masks.

Rather than using tanks or oxygen rebreathers, which were in short supply, UDT swimmers porpoised along, grabbing a breath of air as they could between mortar rounds and machine gun fire. Scouting parties carried fishline for measuring distances and often painted black rings on their bodies at 12-inch intervals for taking shallow-water soundings. Aspirants for service as "frogmen" (a silly term coined by a noncombatant) had to be in top physical condition, capable of swimming 2 miles at a stretch. They also had to remain unshaken by sudden loud noises. On returning home after the war, many former UDT men who could still stand the sight of water returned to the sea, taking up diving as a sport. Once more donning face masks, they attracted other water lovers whose fascination became all-consuming with their first clear glimpse beneath the surface. As hunters, they enjoyed breath-hold diving (skin diving) in coastal shoals, lakes, and quarries, where their prey could be shallow-water fish or shellfish.

Despite Xerxes, Alexander the Great, Italian charioteers, and American demolition teams, warfare has not been the sole mover of man's underwater efforts. During the forties in France free dives with Aqua-Lungs had been made to increasing depths for the purposes of equipment testing, underwater film making, cave exploring, and pure curiosity. Frederick Dumas went to 203 feet; Jacques Cousteau and others (Farques, Georges, Morandiere, Tailliez) dived to 297 feet; and Dumas later descended to 307 feet. Riding on the wave of its success, the Aqua-Lung was marketed commercially in France in 1946. It appeared in Great Britain in 1950, in Canada in 1951, and in the United States a year later. One of the first two units to be brought to the United States was received eagerly at the Scripps Institution of Oceanography in California. With their first tank dive, marine researchers recognized the Aqua-Lung as an invaluable tool for the ocean scientist and a boon to the sport diver.

Many refinements have been made in simplifying self-contained breathing apparatus, but the principle has remained basically the same. Gone from the diving scene is the original two-hose regulator, replaced by the more efficient single-hose system. Steel tanks, long the hallmark of scuba diving, now rank second to aluminum cylinders, which offer greater corrosion protection and hold much more air for their size. Closed-circuit systems, which use oxygen as a breathing medium, and semi-closed scuba, which uses a mixed gas supply, are being perfected and may some day become available to the recreation diver. Microchip technology has produced instruments that can monitor diving time, depth, and decompression status. Some even give readouts of tank air. Lightweight, form-fitting diving suits provide good thermal protection and permit free body movement. Diving is not a static sport.

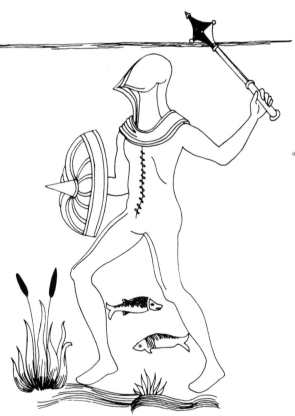

Club, shield, and helmet prepare a brave warrior to do blind battle beneath the surface of the sea. Many of the early woodcuts and drawings of diving were fabrications of a lively imagination fired by humanity's age-old desire to move easily about underwater.

2

The Safe Diver

Fitness and Training

Diving is a vigorous sport, a demanding activity that calls for a healthy body and a healthy mind. It is not a sport for the pack-and-a-half-of-cigarettes-a-day person who can't walk up the front steps without puffing, nor is it for the scatter-brain who has a hard time remembering which hand is which.

Diving requires a degree of physical exertion comparable to that put forth in running and a level of concentration equivalent to what you'd need in flying an airplane. Anything less will make you a hazard to yourself and a handicap to anyone near you. Only when you are in good physical and mental condition can you handle yourself properly and safely as a diver and derive maximum pleasure from exploring the underwater world.

BEING PHYSICALLY FIT

If you are grossly overweight, smoke excessively, or drink like a fish instead of swimming like one, you may do well to take up some other sport. However, if you're not in good physical shape, yet are determined to dive, you had best do something about changing your way of living before you

23

begin, so that it won't be changed for you rather unpleasantly after you've started. Skin and scuba diving do not require that you be an Olympic-caliber swimmer, nor do you have to be as hefty as a weightlifter. What is more important than either swimming prowess or sheer muscular strength is being in *good* shape. This means having good stamina and good wind and being able to carry on under sometimes less than ideal conditions. Cold water, the effects of humidity and pressure, and pure physical exertion demand a level of fitness considerably above the requirements of general recreational activity. Because your condition is the one thing you can control, it should be one thing you can depend on.

There are no hard-and-fast rules for defining diving fitness. If you're an active hiker or jogger, if you can play a fast game of tennis or bike hard without being ruined for the rest of the day, you should have little trouble with your heart and lungs in diving. A regular exercise program of running or swimming has proved to be a fine conditioner and will help maintain a good state of diving fitness.

Any number of tests are available for evaluating fitness, and the better tests take into account an individual's age, weight, and everyday activities. Sport/fitness facilities are to be found throughout the country, even in the smallest communities. Instructors or exercise specialists can test your aerobic capabilities, your strength, and your flexibility, as well as evaluate your overall fitness level from the standpoint of the physiological demands of the sport of your choice. But perhaps the greatest benefits resulting from a steady program of exercise are a sense of well-being and reduced tensions.

A word about overweight divers. Fat absorbs nitrogen (one of the key constituents of the air you breathe from your scuba tank) five times faster than do other body tissues. Dissolved nitrogen causes the diving disease known as the bends. Therefore, overweight people are likely candidates for the bends. The U.S. Navy's decompression tables—essential for diving deep safety—are based on an average weight and build. If you're a fatty, or out of shape in other ways, you're diving with a handicap.

Smoking, Drinking, Drugs

Scuba diving demands that the respiratory system always be in top working order, capable of getting the most out of every breath of air. Divers who smoke are not only subjecting themselves to the long-term chances of cancer but are also tarring the insides of their lungs with poisons that inhibit the proper diffusion of oxygen to the body. Smoking causes irritants to build up in the air passages and thus affects the normal respiratory process of smooth inhalation and exhalation. Steady smokers are familiar with "that ticklish feeling" in the back of the throat, a sensation that can be sensational if it triggers a coughing fit when you're 30 feet below the surface.

What about diving while under the influence of alcohol or drugs? If the underwater world is such an enthralling place, won't it become even more so when one's perceptions are sharpened? The reasoning may be sound, but the facts are quite the opposite. Initially a stimulant, alcohol quickly becomes a depressant. It causes loss in body heat; dulls initiative, awareness, and judgment; and at depth induces nausea.

Marijuana used before diving has been shown to be equally hazardous, causing an intolerance to cold water, a reduction in breath-holding capability, general discomfort, lethargy, and irritability. Again, judgment and common sense fall by the wayside, and the ability to make decisions is impaired in the fuzzy world of artificial stimulation. The underwater world is indeed a world of wonder, but you need a fit body and a clear mind to appreciate it fully.

Fringe Benefits of a Medical Examination

Whatever your age or condition, a physical examination before starting diving is a good idea. You may be the picture of glowing health and feel great, but when a physician gives you a going-over, you both may learn something about your body that you didn't realize before. For example, you may be subject to respiratory blockages that, in your daily life, are insignificant, but that could be of major importance when it comes to breathing compressed air at depth. Your heart may be sturdy enough for normal activities, even for lively land-side sports, but it may not be up to the physical strains of moving your entire body around under pressures four or five times greater than normal.

After a major operation, a prolonged illness, or a severe cold, you should have a repeat checkup. Anyone suffering from asthma, chronic allergies, susceptibility to ear infections, or perforated eardrums should discuss the matter with a doctor, and perhaps with a qualified diving instructor as well. All this is not meant to paint a gloomy picture or to be a deterrent. The potential diver who is blessed with enthusiasm and a sense of wonder—even adventure—is fortunate. The potential diver who is also physically fit, possesses common sense, and has a regard for the well-being of other divers is a "good" diver before even entering the water.

MENTAL FITNESS IS A STATE OF MIND

A person's psychological fitness for diving is a difficult area to evaluate, and often *you* are more capable of judging your mental well-being than a doctor is. Evaluating yourself, however, requires complete honesty and a willingness to admit to fears or uncertainties; if you deceive yourself, you're doing more harm than good. As a diver you may be timid and careful, but you should also have enough self-assurance to be able to handle an unexpected situation in a calm, collected manner. You should possess a keen awareness of the world about you, having almost a sixth sense of what is happening or about to happen. You should be able to recognize early symptoms of fatigue in yourself and your buddy. You should be alert to subtle changes in currents, waves, and depth, and be ready to react to them. You should be able to think ahead and be open to modifying a plan if conditions warrant it. And remember that self-confidence is one thing but bullheadedness is something else. Everyone likes to be right, but a stubborn insistence on being right may make a diver dead wrong.

As big as the ocean is, there's no room in it for a reckless diver. The devil-may-care personality may look thrilling on a TV screen, but in real life a responsible diver doesn't take risks. He isn't a hotshot. Getting himself and his buddy in and out of the water safely is of prime importance, and there just isn't enough time for showing off.

A curious characteristic of diving, noted initially by beginners and repeatedly by advanced divers, is its tendency to be completely absorbing. Both in the training pool and in open water, divers are totally taken up by the activity of diving, the marvel of being underwater. For a period they find themselves putting aside all cares, all thoughts of anything not connected with what they are doing. Diving is one of those rare activities that enrich life.

DIVING FITNESS AND SWIMMING ABILITY

Any diving course worth its salt includes a basic swimming test whose purpose is two-fold. Usually given to beginning student divers in a swimming pool at the first meeting, it provides the instructor an opportunity to observe how the students handle themselves in the water, and it lets *them* know what kind of swimming shape they're in. The specifics may vary from instructor to instructor, but the following six skills are a good test of diving fitness and water ability.

1. Swim fifteen minutes nonstop, demonstrating the flutter kick, frog

kick, and scissors kick (or using the crawl, backstroke, breaststroke, and side-stroke).

    2. Swim 50 feet underwater, without fins and without push-off.

    3. Retrieve a 10-pound weight from the bottom at a depth of 10 to 15 feet.

    4. Swim 100 feet while wearing a 5- to 8-pound weight belt.

    5. Tow an inert swimmer 50 yards without fins.

    6. Demonstrate the proper technique for survival float (see the following section).

Failing any of these qualifications isn't going to flunk you out before you begin, but passing all of them indicates mastery of the high degree of watermanship needed to be a safe diver. Falling short on any indicates a need for further basic swimming conditioning.

DROWNPROOFING—SURVIVAL IN THE WATER

Drownproofing is a method of remaining afloat for hours while expending a minimum amount of movement and energy. Since 1963, when drownproofing was developed by Fred Lanoue, swimming coach at Georgia Institute of Technology, hundreds of educational institutions and swimming and diving clubs have included the technique as a part of their aquatic program. The method presumes that nearly all men and women can be taught to float, inasmuch as the density of the human body is nearly that of water and even a totally submerged body will have some buoyancy. Treading water works for a little while, but because most people tend to float vertically, considerable expenditure of heat and energy is needed to keep the head out of the water over a long period of time. Drownproofing works on the principle of breathing rhythmically and letting the head sink underwater for a rest between breaths. The method takes into account both good and poor floaters and allows for traveling at a slow, easy rate. Practice the techniques first in a swimming pool, then, when you feel confident, in open, calm water. Remember that the key to drownproofing is relaxation.

A   **B**   **C**

STAY-AFLOAT TECHNIQUE FOR GOOD FLOATERS

First take a breath through your mouth while hanging completely relaxed in a vertical position, arms and legs dangling (A). Let yourself sink under the surface.

Now float up, which you will do, owing to the air in your lungs. When your head is partly out of the water, raise your arms straight out to the side while stretching one leg forward and the other back as if getting ready for a scissors kick (B).

Gently bring your arms down and your legs together. As soon as your arms start down (not shown), begin to exhale through your nose (C) and continue to do so until your nose is above the surface. Be sure your chin is on the surface, not above. Once your mouth is above water, take a breath.

D

E

F

Again let yourself sink and, just as your head goes under, give a slight downward push with your arms to avoid going too deep (D). (This extra push won't be necessary in calm water, but you should learn how to do it because you may go a little deeper when wearing diving gear.)

Rest underwater again, completely relaxed (E). Remain submerged only until you desire a breath, not until you need one. (At first you'll probably stay under for about three seconds, which should be the minimum, but you must gradually increase your submerged rest time. The average rest after doing the exercise for an hour is ten seconds.)

Repeat the entire cycle (F), remembering that relaxation is the key to successful floating.

A

B

C

STAY-AFLOAT TECHNIQUE FOR POOR FLOATERS

First take a breath and relax, arms and legs dangling, neck loose, head tilting forward slightly. The back of your head should protrude a little from the water (A). If your rear end swings up, you have taken too big a breath and should exhale a little air through your nose.

As you slowly float up, raise your arms in front of you. Bring one knee up, then extend that leg forward. At the same time, raise your other foot behind you and extend that leg back (B). Don't lift your head, and don't raise your arms or legs too fast, or you may go deeper.

With your legs extended front and back and your arms out in front, quickly raise your head out of the water, stopping with your chin still in the water (C). As you bring your head up, exhale through your nose.

D

E

F

The instant your head becomes vertical, sweep your arms out and down and step gently downward with both feet, bringing your legs together (D). Be careful that these strokes are not too fast or vigorous or you'll pop too far out of the water and go under again too soon. When your face is above the surface, take a breath through your mouth.

Relax and again let yourself sink (E). In rough water, or if wearing clothing, unless you drop your head forward as soon as it is under the surface and make a downward stroke with your arms or legs, you will sink too far.

Repeat the entire cycle (F).

A **B** **C**

TRAVEL STROKE

First float easily with your head above the water, your arms dangling relaxed (A).

Inhale and let yourself go completely below the surface. As soon as your head slips under, tip your face down and bring your arms up and out in front. Prepare for a scissors kick by bringing one leg forward and the other back, raising your rear foot as high as you can (B).

Bring your legs together and, as soon as the scissors kick is completed, bring your arms down (C).

D

E

F

As your hands tough your thighs, you will glide toward the surface at an angle. Be sure to keep your head down and forward and your body in a straight line (D). During the glide, exhale slightly but never completely. (How much you should exhale is learned only through practice.)

When you want a breath, begin to return to a vertical position by drawing both knees up toward your chest. Round your back and extend your hands forward and up toward your face (E).

Extend one leg forward in preparation for a scissors kick without letting the other knee go back, keeping your arms out in front of you. When your trunk is nearly vertical, raise your head above the surface and press gently downward with the sole of your front foot and both hands (F). This will support you while you take a breath. Then repeat the entire cycle.

FORMAL TRAINING AND CERTIFICATION

One of the greatest problems faced by the diving fraternity is the untrained diver. Anyone can pick up the rudiments of diving from a friend, and anyone can strap on a scuba tank and move around underwater. Many survive the experience and even repeat it.

      Formal training means training according to a structured course by a qualified instructor. Formal training assures your being offered a planned program of basic theory and tested practical instruction. What you get from such training depends wholly on your attitude, but at least you are exposed to the proper "why" and "how to" of diving. A certification card with your name on it is no evidence that you're a good diver, but it does indicate that you've had the opportunity to learn diving fundamentals the right way. Let's see what goes into a typical course of instruction.

NAUI certification cards indicate varied training and levels of proficiency. Other instructional organizations issue similar certifications. Conscientious dive shop operators will not sell air or rent equipment to uncertified divers.

Whether you sign up for a skin and scuba course in school, with the YMCA, or at a dive shop, you'll receive pretty much the same basic instruction. Any qualified civilian instructor in the United States will have probably been trained —and trained well—by one of this country's recognized diving organizations: National Association of Underwater Instructors (NAUI), National Association of Skin Diving Schools (NASDS), Professional Association of Diving Instructors (PADI), Scuba Schools International (SSI), YMCA, or Los Angeles County Department of Parks and Recreation, one of the very best regional training groups.

You will have a minimum of thirty-six hours of instruction, made up of classroom lectures and water time with at least four open-water dives using skills learned in a swimming pool. Your introductory course will cover the following topics:

Watermanship	Beach and boat entries and exits
Use of equipment	Safety skills and special skills
Skin and scuba skills	Marine life
Basic physics and gas laws	Rescue and first aid
Diving maladies	Use of dive tables
Surface and underwater swimming	

Advanced Diver Training

After your basic or open-water course, and after putting some open-water hours behind you, you may want to learn some of the more sophisticated diving skills. Most advanced scuba courses require basic certification or demonstration of superior diving ability. An advanced course usually contains sixteen hours of practical, in-water instruction and sixteen classroom hours covering the following:

Applied science	Night diving
Basic skills review	Search and recovery
Equipment review	Light salvage
Lifesaving and first aid	Deep diving
Underwater navigation	Advanced skills
Limited visibility diving	

Remember that fitness is no guarantee you'll be a good diver. Furthermore, no course, no instructor, can make you a safe diver. However much you are exposed to the skills and the proper techniques of diving, what you do with the knowledge and training is up to you.

Curious diver and curious fish stalk one another around delicate red gorgonia at 70-foot depth off California's Channel Islands.

3

Snorkel, Suit, and Scuba

Choosing and Using the Right Equipment

The underwater world is a spellbinding world, quite unlike any other. It is a world in which you, as a diver, will experience new freedoms of movement, new physical sensations, new emotions. Yet the very equipment enabling these experiences imposes certain limitations that take a little getting used to by one who has always walked about on dry land. As yet, man cannot remain underwater long without a constant supply of air; he cannot see without a captive bubble of air in front of his eyes; he cannot maintain even body temperature without some form of insulation.

THE GEAR THAT GOES ON YOUR BODY

Although diving technology has advanced at an accelerated rate over the last decade and apparatus is constantly being made more compact, a fully equipped scuba diver may wear and carry into the water in excess of sixty pounds. Most of that weight is taken up by the life-support system —the air supply, the protective suit, the propulsion system—and thus is essential. Learning how

37

to use this basic equipment without discomfort, until you hardly realize that you have it on, is the mark of the skilled diver—the safe diver.

Face Masks and Snorkels

The naked human eye, which perceives with such clarity in open air, is virtually blind underwater. Forms and masses can be vaguely made out, but without a layer of air separating the eyes from water contact, objects are little more than blurred shapes. The face mask is designed to retain a bubble of air in front of the eyes, enabling the diver to see as clearly as water conditions permit. Face mask shape and style are a matter of individual preference; a great many types are available, but the prime requirement is that a mask keep air in and water out. You must choose a mask that fits your own facial configuration. In selecting one, hold it against your face and gently inhale through your nose without pulling the strap over your head. If you can breathe any air in around the rubber flange, the fit is not a good one. For a watertight fit you should feel the mask push snugly against your face, and it should stay in place until you exhale.

Face masks are available in a variety of styles and shapes to fit any personal taste or facial configuration. A good mask has a tempered glass lens secured by a metal retaining ring, a broad adjustable head strap, and a soft rubber skirt. Prescription mask, lower left, has built-in lenses.

A good mask is made of strong but pliable rubber or silicone. The lens or faceplate should not be plastic, which scratches, but shatterproof, clear glass, held by a sturdy, noncorrosive frame. Some masks have one-way exhaust valves under or in front of the nose, useful for purging water. Some have nose-pinching devices, which help equalize pressure in the ears.

Although a few divers wear contact lenses inside their masks, they run the risk of losing them if the mask becomes flooded or knocked off. Some opticians specialize in grinding prescription lenses which they cement inside a mask. In addition to the price of the mask, you can expect to pay about seventy-five dollars for such customizing. If you're the hairy type, with a handlebar mustache, you may have to wiggle the mask around on your face a bit to get a good seal to your upper lip. Don't make the head strap too tight or you'll give yourself a headache. It should hold the mask snugly to your face but not so snugly that it cuts into your forehead.

Every dive shop sells antifogging preparations, and, like a sure cure for hiccups, every diver has a special trick for keeping the inside of a mask clear of condensation. Perhaps the best way is also the simplest. Just before donning your mask, spit into it, rub the saliva around on the inside of the glass, then rinse.

Divers occasionally use silicone grease to lubricate zippers and to help preserve the rubber of masks and fins. If you get any of this on the faceplate, you won't be able to unfog your mask until you wash the silicone off the glass with soap and water.

Goggles are not recommended for diving. They don't permit underwater pressure on the eyes to be equalized and can cause ruptured blood vessels in the eyes, a malady that looks as bad as it sounds.

A snorkel is a J-shaped tube with a mouthpiece at the short end. It enables you to breathe easily while surface swimming face down in the water. Not having to raise your head for a breath allows you to keep a constant visual scan of the bottom, to look for fish, shallows, or good diving spots. A snorkel is invaluable when you have no air left in your scuba tank and have to make the long swim home on the surface.

Snorkels are made of plastic or rubber. The one you use should have a pliable mouthpiece that fits your bite comfortably and does not rub against the roof of your mouth or chafe your gums. The most efficient snorkels are simple tubes with a minimum of bends to impede air flow; they have large diameters and are short in length (about 12 inches). Avoid attachments designed to keep water out of your snorkel or help purge it. These gimmicks often leak and slow

A good snorkel has a large-bore barrel for breathing ease, a comfortable mouthpiece, and a minimum of bends. A strip of reflecting tape on the tip makes spotting a diver at the surface easier. The figure-eight loops secure the snorkel to the face mask strap.

down your swimming. It's better to learn how to use a simple snorkel properly than to depend on questionable gadgets.

Snorkels should be attached to the left side of your mask strap with a keeper—a piece of neoprene shaped like a figure eight (in a pinch you can use a heavy rubber band). Why on the left? So it won't interfere with your scuba regulator mouthpiece, the hose of which comes around the right side of your head.

Swim Fins

A swim fin is a kind of ungainly looking but beautifully efficient duck's foot. Swim fins give added thrust and help you move efficiently through the water. The stiffer type of fin provides greater power but requires a greater expenditure of energy, whereas a flexible fin offers less water resistance but also gives less thrust. Most fins that are black are denser than water and do not float. Most colored fins float and thus are easier to find if they come off in the water.

Though no fin is known for being easy to walk in, the closed-heel version gives some foot protection against rocks and coral; however, it does tend to get knocked off in surf. Closed-heel fins usually come in shoe sizes, are fairly easy to fit, and are generally more comfortable than open-heel types, which have an adjustable strap and feel more secure on the feet but are made only in small, medium, and large sizes. The choice of open- or closed-heel is a matter of personal preference.

If your fins cause cramps across your arches, the foot pocket is too small, the strap is too tight, or you are not conditioned to the fins. If you get cramps in your calf or thigh muscles, the fins may be too stiff for you. If you expect to wear wet suit booties with your open heel fins, make sure the straps are adjusted so that the fins can be pulled on and slipped off without too much strain.

When you don fins, they'll go on easier if you wet them first. Loose strap ends may catch in aquatic weeds, so wrap them securely with black plastic tape. To keep from losing a fin in the surf, you may want to purchase Y-shaped straps, or else extra-long straps that wind around your ankle and snap down.

Swim fins are the principal means of locomotion underwater or at the surface. Top four are large-bladed fins with an adjustable heel. At bottom right is a closed heel, non-adjustable fin, useful in areas with coral or sea urchins.

Protective Suits

Your normal body temperature is 98.6° F. and, whenever you are submerged in water even a few degrees lower, heat transfers from you to your surrounding. When diving in cold water, or when submerged for long periods of time even in relatively warm water, heat drains away from your body surprisingly fast and some kind of thermal protection is essential. When you begin to feel a chill, you should get out of the water, or else surface and breathe deeply a few times to get warmer air into your lungs. If you allow yourself to get so cold that you're numb or have the shakes, you're liable to get into trouble because you are not in complete control of yourself. The best way to delay loss of body heat is to wear a protective suit.

Wet suits are usually made of neoprene, a synthetic-rubber foam consisting of millions of tiny air cells. A wet suit doesn't keep you dry but allows a thin layer of water to lie next to your skin. This layer is warmed by your body heat, and the foam insulates it—and hence you—from the colder surrounding water.

Wet suits are manufactured in several thicknesses: ⅛, ³⁄₁₆, ¼, ⅜, and even ½ inch. The colder the water and the longer the dive, the thicker the suit should be. Not all thicknesses will be available in any one section of the country, so consult dive shops in your area about the proper thickness for the kind of diving you expect to do. Along much of the West Coast, ¼-inch Farmer John suits (suspender-style) are popular throughout the year. Lakes and quarries in most parts of the country warm up during the summer, so thinner suits can be used there, and in temperate waters you may need only a wet jacket rather than a full suit.

To be an effective insulator, a wet suit must fit snugly. If there are air pockets between your shoulder blades, under your arms, or in your crotch, you'll experience shockingly cold flashes as unwarmed water enters and sloshes about next to your skin. When buying a wet suit, shop around to try various makes and styles. If you're lucky enough to find a good fit in a ready-made one, you'll save a few dollars over what you'll pay to have one custom made.

Nylon on both the inside and the outside of a suit is often the sign of a higher quality, custom-made job; it helps keep rips and tears from developing and makes a suit easier to get in and out of. If you're the underwater explorer type and like to crawl along the bottom or over rocks, you might consider putting patches on the knees of your suit. Small points of damage on any suit are easily patched with neoprene cement and scraps of wet-suit material. For total protection in cold water, you should wear neoprene booties, a hood, and gloves or mitts. When wearing a hood, be sure the flange on your face mask fits *inside* the hood's face opening, or you'll have water leaking into the mask.

Because neoprene is made up of air cells, a wet suit will make you float like a cork unless you offset its buoyancy with a weight belt. On the other hand, the deeper you go, the more the air cells in your suit will be flattened by increasing pressure, which will both lessen its insulating properties and decrease its buoyancy.

Dry suits are very popular, especially with cold-water divers, and you can choose from fabric suits, neoprene suits, or vulcanized suits that combine both natural and synthetic rubbers. A dry suit is designed to keep water away from the skin, and by wearing wool or thermal underwear under one, you will stay not only dry but warm. Ice divers sometimes wear a wet suit under a dry suit for maximum thermal protection. The combination is cumbersome but comfortable. Because dry suits are very different from wet suits, you should familiarize yourself with your buoyancy and weight changes by wearing the dry suit in a swimming pool before venturing into open water with it.

Such standard protective suits are only marginally effective under extreme conditions—such as when diving in polar regions—and efforts are constantly being made to develop more efficient means of maintaining body heat. Experiments have been made with electrically warmed suits and hot-water suits, but a trouble-free heated suit for the sport diver is yet to be marketed.

One of the newest types of exposure suits is a one-piece neoprene outfit that includes booties and hood. A coupling on the suit connects a hose to your scuba regulator, and by pressing a button you admit air into the suit. In addition to providing insulation, such a system gives buoyancy control. The air intake button lets air in, making you more buoyant; an exhaust button lets air out and allows you to descend at a controlled rate. This is a very warm suit—usually too warm, except for ice diving or prolonged deep dives.

Weight Belts

Weight belts are normally made up of several lead weights strung onto a nylon web strap. Their purpose is to offset the body's natural buoyancy or to compensate for the increased buoyancy of a wet suit. Weights are seldom needed for diving without a wet suit, but many divers prefer wearing a few pounds in order to sink rapidly while skin diving or to compensate for the buoyant tendencies of their scuba cylinder. One- or two-pound cylindrical weights give better balance and stability than larger ones. If you don't need much weight on your

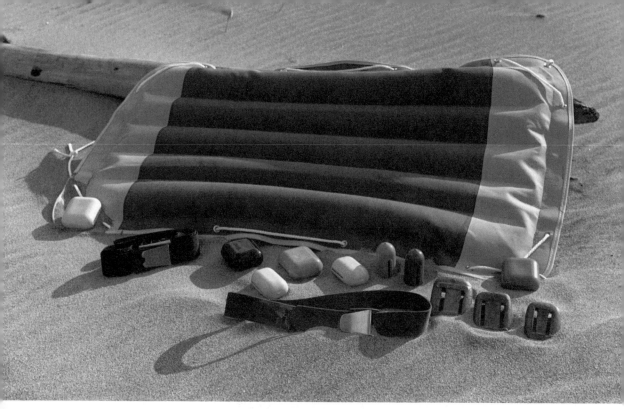

Air mattress, weights, and weight belts. An air mattress allows a diver to kick-float over marine vegetation and to rest above water. Weights offset the body's natural buoyancy, allowing a diver to sink and maneuver easily beneath the surface. Various types of weights are available, from 1½-pound plastic covered units to 5-pound lead blocks.

belt, try to arrange the weights over your hips and use "keepers" to prevent them from sliding around.

A weight belt should have a positive quick-release buckle and should be worn over all other gear so it can be quickly jettisoned with one hand and drop free. Because your weight belt should be the first piece of equipment ditched in the event of an emergency, it should go on last to be sure of clearing anything else when released. Put it on the same way every time, pointing the buckle in the same direction so you can always associate it with a given hand movement. Avoid tying or tucking in strap ends, so that you don't defeat the purpose of the quick-release buckle.

The amount of weighting you'll need depends on your body size, body weight, bone structure, and wet-suit buoyancy. Generally you can figure on wearing one pound for every ten pounds of body weight.

Buoyancy Compensator Vests

Whether skin or scuba diving, you'll find a personal flotation vest, or buoyancy compensator vest, to be an integral part of your equipment. Made of rubber, plastic, or nylon, a BC vest is less a lifesaving device than it is a versatile aid to resting on the surface, compensating for improper weighting, offsetting buoyancy changes on deeper dives, and neutralizing the weight of a full game bag. Handy though it is, a BC vest must never be thought of as a substitute for watermanship or physical fitness.

The ideal vest is full length; it reaches from the neck all the way to the waist without covering the quick release buckles. It goes on easily and is worn comfortably, not interfering with other gear and not riding up when inflated. It is easily inflated, either orally or by means of the scuba tank or a CO_2 cartridge. Oral inflators should have a mouthpiece similar to that on a snorkel, with a good-sized opening. It's a bit comical, and somewhat distressing, to be

Buoyancy compensator vests, or stabilizer jackets, are not life saving devices such as boaters wear. Their purpose is to support a diver at the surface and to help maintain neutral buoyancy at depth. All three jackets shown have auto inflators as well as oral inflators.

trying to blow air into a tiny orifice when your lips are numb and your teeth are chattering.

If the oral inflator hose attaches to the lower portion of the vest instead of at the top, you'll have a hard time getting all the air out when you want to descend, and your buoyancy will be affected. The hose should connect at the very top, behind the neck. Some vests connect to the scuba regulator and are inflated or deflated merely by pressing a button.

A good vest has an overinflation safety valve on the front (usually a round, black fixture about 2 inches in diameter) to release some of the air in the vest when it expands on ascent. Periodically check this valve by inflating the vest to its maximum capacity and pressing it firmly against your body with your hands. The valve should let excess pressure escape.

After each use, drain any small amounts of water that may have gotten into your vest during inflation, put a little air into it, rinse it, and hang it in a well-ventilated place to dry inside and out. Before storing, remove the CO_2 cartridge and lubricate the activator mechanism with silicone spray. It's a good idea to inspect your vest periodically for cracks, tears, or even pinhole leaks, which can be fixed with patching material.

Divers' Knives

The diver's knife is not a weapon but a very handy tool that can be useful in prying, digging, chipping, or freeing yourself of underwater entanglements. One edge should be sharp for cutting marine growth, monofilament line, or even lightweight metal line; the other, sawtoothed for cutting through rope.

The idea is not to swim around with a knife in your hand, like a shark fighter in an old movie, but to have it handy in case you ever need it. To lessen the chance of snagging it, keep it in a scabbard attached to the *inside* of one leg, below the knee. You may never unsheathe your knife except to clean and dry it after a dive, but you never know when you may have to cut yourself away from a length of loose fishing line or a piece of net.

BREATHING APPARATUS

Open-circuit scuba involves inhaling air from a high-pressure cylinder through a mouthpiece connected to a valve system that regulates its flow, and exhaling into the surrounding water. Improvements are constantly being made in scuba

Divers' knives are not razor sharp because they are all-purpose tools rather than weapons. A heavy-duty knife should have a stainless steel blade, a serrated edge for sawing, a contoured grip that feels comfortable in the hand, and a metal handle end for pounding. Many knife blades have a measuring scale for checking the size of game.

equipment, but the basic components remain the same: a tank of compressed air and a regulator.

Compressed Air Tanks

A diving cylinder, or compressed air tank, holds a quantity of air under high pressure. This air supply enables you to stay underwater for longer than you can hold your breath. Most air tanks are made of steel or of aluminum alloys. Steel tanks that are properly cared for will give many years of service; aluminum tanks last almost indefinitely, since they are corrosion resistant.

All cylinders manufactured in the United States carry either a Department of Transportation (DOT) or an Interstate Commerce Commission (ICC)

An aluminum tank with a ¾-inch K valve. The code translates as follows: DOT stands for Department of Transportation; SP6498 is the manufacturer's code for the tank material; 3,000 is the pressure test; P113331 is the tank serial number; USD is the manufacturer's logotype; 3 76 is the month and year of manufacture; L36 in a circle is a dive shop identification.

stamp of approval near the top of the tank, just below the neck. This is accompanied by numbers giving the cylinder's rated pressure, which may vary from 1,800 to 3,000 pounds per square inch (psi), the manufacturer's symbol, a serial number, and the date of manufacture.

The most widely used tanks are the steel 71.2 cubic feet, which are rated at 2250 psi when new, and the aluminum 80 cubic feet, which are rated at 3000 psi.

Individual preference dictates the type of cylinder a diver uses. Just remember that the larger the tank the greater the air capacity, but also the greater the weight.

Annually from the original date of manufacture, a tank should be taken to a dive shop for internal corrosion inspection. Every five years it must, by law, undergo a hydrostatic test, in which it is subjected to an excess of internal pressure for the purpose of detecting leaks or structural weaknesses. Because a fully charged scuba tank contains a force of more than a ton, it is in effect a bomb and should be handled and cared for with due respect. Internal corrosion can eat away the sidewalls of a steel tank until they are so weak that the tank may explode. Having a tank visually inspected and hydrostatted is *your* responsibility—no one else's. As a safe diver you should keep up a regular preventive maintenance schedule for a diving tank just as you would for your car.

Scuba tanks should have an inside visual inspection once a year to check for corrosion. They must, by law, undergo a hydrostatic test every five years from the manufacturer's date. Hydrostatting subjects a tank to pressure in excess of its rated value in order to test its wall strength. From left to right: aluminum 80 cubic feet, aluminum 67 cubic feet, steel 95 cubic feet, and steel 60 cubic feet.

When transporting a tank, lay it on its side and tie or block it securely so it doesn't roll around. Also protect the neck and valve assembly by wrapping them with a thick towel. An exploding tank can blow out the side of a car or go through the wall of a building, destroying anything in its path. Be especially careful with your tank when suiting up for a dive. Don't just stand it up and expect it to stay there. Either lay it on its side, with the valve protected, or set it upright with its bottom sunk several inches in the sand to prevent its being accidentally toppled. If you plan to store your scuba tank for a long period, keep an internal pressure of about 100 psi (some pressure is needed to keep moisture out). Put it away in a cool place, blocked upright so it won't be knocked over.

Even small amounts of water in a scuba tank can cause corrosion and thus shorten the tank's life. Moisture can enter by (1) allowing a tank to be drained of all air and letting it sit with its valve open; (2) draining a tank of air and purging the regulator underwater; (3) water's being blown in through the valve orifice during filling.

A scuba tank should be worn on a sturdy backpack equipped with a nylon strap harness and a quick-release buckle. When putting on a tank and harness for the first time, adjust the straps to fit your shoulders and midsection snugly but not too tightly. A too-tight harness will restrict both movement and breathing.

Tank Valves

Protruding from the neck of a scuba cylinder is a shiny, squarish affair with a knob on one side and an orifice surrounded by a black rubber gasket, called an "O" ring, in the other. This is the tank valve, which, when opened by being turned counterclockwise, allows air to flow to the regulator or permits air to be put into the tank. Most tank valves have a built-in safety device in the form of a thin metal disc designed to rupture at excessive cylinder pressure or high heat, thus preventing tank explosion.

There are two types of tank valves: the standard kind (called a "K" valve) and the constant-reserve kind (called a "J" valve). A "K" valve is simply an on-off system that works much like a water faucet to open and close the high-pressure orifice. When it's open, you get air; when it's closed, you don't.

The constant-reserve ("J") valve is an additional, spring-loaded device that cuts off your air supply gradually when the cylinder pressure gets down to about 300 psi, in effect holding that amount of air in reserve until you turn down a small lever. When breathing gets hard, you switch to reserve—usually by pulling down a rod located at the side of the tank. Whenever you go on

Submersible depth and pressure gauges are available in varied quality, accuracy, performance, and price. Pressure gauges attach to the high-pressure stage of a regulator, allowing a diver to read available air in the tank. A depth gauge such as the one on the far left can be worn on the wrist or mounted in a console. Some consoles also contain dive timers and compasses.

reserve you should terminate your dive, using the remaining air to surface and exit from the water.

Although "J" valves are widely used, many divers prefer a nonreserve system with an attached submersible pressure gauge that allows them to monitor the air remaining in their tank constantly. A pressure gauge can be used with a constant-reserve system, but at low pressures it is effective only if the valve lever is kept in the "down" or open position.

At one time, a submersible pressure gauge was considered an optional piece of gear. Divers accustomed to using a constant-reserve valve seldom looked at a gauge even if it was on the scuba equipment they were using. However, because a gauge is the only sure way of monitoring the air supply, the safety-minded diver should consider it an essential instrument.

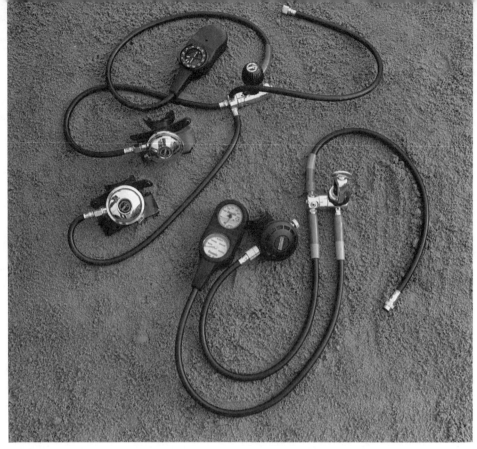

Regulators reduce the scuba tank's air pressure to a breathable level. The octopus regulator at the top has two second stages, allowing two divers to share a common source of air in an emergency.

Regulators

A regulator is a mechanical system that supplies air to the diver from the high-pressure tank as it is needed. A regulator consists of a mouthpiece, a hose, and one or two pressure-reducing units (called "stages").

Though still favored by a few veteran divers, double-hose regulators are gradually being phased out of production. In a two-hose regulator the hose on the right carries air to the diver; the one on the left carries exhaled air to the water chamber in back of the head. With this system, bubbles are exhausted behind the head rather than in front of the face. This is a plus for the underwater photographer but a small blessing in comparison with the lower cost and simplicity of the single-hose arrangement.

Single-hose regulators are more compact. No exhalation hose is needed, since the exhaust valve is attached directly to the mouthpiece. High-pressure reduction takes place in the tank valve, and air at a breathable pressure then goes to the demand regulator attached to the mouthpiece. As long as the tank has air in it the hose cannot fill with water, and any water that might get into the mouthpiece is easily cleared by pressing a purge button.

All single-hose regulators are two-stage, which means they have two steps of tank pressure reduction separated by an intermediate-pressure hose. The first stage is the solid-feeling cylindrical unit that attaches to the tank valve. It reduces the 2,250 to 3,000 psi tank pressure to 120 to 140 psi. The second stage is the disc-shaped unit on the mouthpiece that houses the demand mechanism which gives a diver a breath of air when he wants—or demands—it, at a pressure balanced with that of the surrounding water, regardless of the depth.

Regulator prices range from about one hundred fifty dollars to two hundred dollars and up. The average sport diver can get a good regulator for around one hundred seventy five dollars, whereas the professional, or someone who dives often throughout the year, may spend considerably more. In choosing a regulator, discuss your needs and underwater interests with diving instructors, experienced divers, and dive shop personnel. Don't overbuy by getting the most expensive unit if you don't need it. And don't purchase by looks rather than capabilities.

Certain special features may be important enough to you to influence your choice. A *high*-pressure port on the first stage lets you attach a submersible tank pressure gauge. A *low*-pressure port on the first stage permits attachment of another hose and second stage to make an octopus rig.

The octopus rig consists of two regulator second stages connected to one regulator first stage, a simple yet significant advancement that lets two divers

Alternate air source. A self-contained emergency air supply, sometimes called an emergency bailout bottle, is preferred by some divers.

share one tank of air in an emergency. Standard regulator hoses are about 24 inches long; an octopus hose is 10 to 12 inches longer, which allows the divers to swim side by side instead of having to face each other. To keep the long octopus out of the way when not in use, secure it to your buoyancy compensator vest with a breakaway clip.

Special Scuba

The type of scuba in widest use is the open-circuit system, in which compressed air is inhaled and carbon dioxide is exhaled directly into the water. With closed-circuit, oxygen-rebreathing equipment, the diver rebreathes oxygen that has passed through a carbon dioxide absorbent. No bubbles are given off, since exhalation remains entirely within the system. Closed-circuit scuba is used chiefly by the military and by professional photographers. Oxygen rebreathers are not commonly available, and this is just as well because they are potentially hazardous rigs and should be used only by someone thoroughly trained and fully aware of their dangers.

Semiclosed-circuit scuba (or mixed-gas scuba) is something of a cross between an open-circuit system and the simple oxygen rebreather. The diver breathes a mixture of nitrogen and oxygen, or helium and oxygen, and the exhaled gas is reclaimed and reused. This type of rig enables longer and deeper dives with safety. As yet, semiclosed-circuit scuba is not widely available, and its cost is in the neighborhood of two thousand dollars. As technology develops, and as greater production brings the cost down, semiclosed scuba may find its way to the corner dive shop.

A hookah rig is sometimes used for prolonged work in shallow water, such as commercial abalone and scallop harvesting, wreck salvage, or scientific study. When using a hookah setup, a diver doesn't wear a compressed air cylinder. Instead, the diver is connected to a cylinder or compressor at the surface and breathes through a full face mask.

MISCELLANEOUS EQUIPMENT

A mask and snorkel, a pair of fins, a weight belt, and a buoyancy compensator vest are essential for skin diving. Add to these an air tank and a regulator and you have the basic gear for scuba diving. Little else in the way of equipment is really necessary for the enjoyment of this most enjoyable activity. However, for particular forms of diving, certain special pieces of gear are recommended.

Depth Gauges

Of little use to the skin diver, who seldom goes deeper than 30 or 50 feet and who never stays there more than a few seconds, a depth gauge is invaluable to scuba divers, who usually need to know how deep they are in order to be able to tell how long their air will last. In murky waters, on night dives, and during deep dives, a depth gauge is an absolute necessity.

Depth gauges range in price from around twenty-five dollars to eighty dollars, or you can spend as much as nine hundred dollars on an electronic dive computer that sets up and remembers a diving profile. Aside from such high-tech devices, there are four basic types of depth gauges: capillary, Bourdon tube, diaphragm, and oil filled.

Whatever your budget, finding a depth gauge to meet it is not difficult. They range in price from around ten to fifty dollars, the higher costs buying greater accuracy and greater depth capability. Four basic types of gauges are commonly found: capillary, Bourdon tube, diaphragm, and oil-filled.

Lowest in price and simplest in principle, a capillary gauge consists of a small plastic tube sealed at one end and open at the other. The tube is formed into a circle and mounted against a calibrated scale. With increasing depth, more water enters the open end, causing the trapped air bubble to become more compressed. The front edge of the water column gives a reading, against the scale, for depth in feet. Capillary gauges are highly accurate, but at depths greater than about 40 feet the movement of the water column is so slight that the increments are difficult to read. Capillary gauges are flat, lightweight, and low in cost. However, they clog easily with sand and silt and thus can become quickly inoperative.

The Bourdon depth gauge consists of a small tube attached to a needle movement, sealed at atmospheric pressure into a compartment. Water enters a surrounding chamber, and increasing pressure creates a differential that distorts the tube, causing the needle to read on a calibrated face. Though more expensive than the capillary type of gauge, because of its moving parts, the Bourdon gauge is very accurate. Sand or salt crystals can plug up its entry port, so it is best used for clear fresh-water diving.

The oil-filled depth gauge has a sealed, oil-filled case: no water enters it. Increasing pressure pushes against the glass front of the gauge, and its distortion is translated to needle movement. Oil-filled gauges are highly accurate at depth but may be off in the 0- to 30-foot range. They respond quickly to changes in depth, some reading to 300 feet.

A diaphragm, or air-filled, depth gauge also has a sealed housing made of rubber or plastic. Increasing pressure depresses a diaphragm, which causes

Electronic dive computers assist a diver in understanding the profile developed for each dive. Such instruments help avoid decompression dives.

movement of a lever and gear assembly connected to a needle, giving a reading on a calibrated face. This type of gauge is expensive but very accurate. When first worn on the wrist it may seem cumbersome, since it is more than 1 inch thick and 2½ inches in diameter.

Tiny batteries and integrated circuitry are used in some depth gauges to give a digital display. The illuminated numbers, which change with changing depth, are clearly seen and easily read, especially in dim light.

Depth gauges should be handled with care and stored in such a way that they won't be bumped or banged around. Abuse can cause them to read inaccurately, a serious matter on deep dives.

Underwater Compasses

An underwater compass is not essential as a safety item for most divers—and certainly not for snorkelers and skin divers. But once you have learned how to use one, you won't make a scuba descent without it. A compass helps you swim the shortest way to a rendezvous or back to your starting point. It extends diving time and helps you conserve energy and air by eliminating the need to surface often to look around. In waters of low visibility, or on night dives, a compass is indispensable. Using a compass properly (see Chapter 6) takes a little practice, but learning how to navigate underwater and how to surface right where you planned is a great delight.

Because a compass is influenced by metallic masses, it should be worn on the right wrist. All other gauges should go on the left wrist.

An underwater compass should be filled with liquid and should have an easy-to-read luminous face and lubber line and a movable bezel that turns easily. After every dive, wash your compass thoroughly with fresh water, rotating the bezel ring to rinse out sand grains or salt crystals.

A diver's compass should be the only instrument worn on the right wrist, to avoid magnetic deflections caused by other metallic objects. For deep diving or night diving, a compass should have a luminous scale, north arrow, lubber line, and rotatable indicator.

Divers' Watches

A diver's watch is needed on deep dives, whether or not decompression is involved; on night dives; and on long-period dives when two or more tanks are worn. It is also invaluable for underwater compass navigation. A watch is not used so much for telling what time it is underwater as for measuring elapsed time.

When shopping for an underwater watch, choose one with luminous, easily read numbers and hands and a nonslipping bezel. Look to the proven name brands that carry a strong guarantee because many low-priced watches will not hold up for long.

Dive watches and timers should have an internal light or luminous numbers that will be visible at depth. Before starting a repetitive dive, make a habit of checking that all moveable dials or depth indicators have been reset to zero.

Dive Computers

Under normal conditions, a man swimming easily at the surface consumes air at the rate of about 1 cubic foot per minute. As he goes deeper, breathing compressed air, increased water pressure causes him to use more air. For example, at 33 feet he will consume 2 cubic feet per minute, and at 66 feet he will use 3 cubic feet. The deeper he goes, the more air he uses, and thus the less time he can stay down on a given amount of air.

A depth-compensating dive timer is a sophisticated instrument that gives a simple visual presentation of minutes of air remaining for any depth and eliminates the necessity of making computations for each dive. Though most sport divers will have little need for such a specialized piece of equipment, it is of great value to professionals.

Technical advances have brought to the sport diver highly accurate instruments that keep track of depth and available air, warn of the requirement for a decompression dive, and advise of the depth at which to decompress. One of these—the electronic dive computer—has caused a revolution in diving.

Diving to 33 feet or less does not necessitate such sophisticated instruments, but, even so, seasoned divers often choose an electronic dive computer as a standard piece of gear to be used on every dive.

Remember that any dive meter or computer is a delicate instrument. Rough treatment can cause it to give false readings, which could result in your experiencing the bends. Since unquestionable trust in a damaged instrument could mean trouble, as a prudent diver you should always use dive tables as a backup.

The Everything Panel

Some manufacturers, concerned with the potential array of gauges required or desired by many divers, have developed a unitized instrumentation system. Integrated into one handy modular panel, or instrument caddy, are a depth gauge, a tank pressure gauge, a compass, a dive timer, and sometimes a decomp meter. One glance in one place gives the diver a wealth of information.

For Diving in Dark Places

The exploration of underwater caves and underground siphons requires all the equipment needed for other forms of diving plus a few special items necessary for safety in a dark and confined environment. A pony bottle is a miniature air cylinder, usually with a capacity of 12 cubic feet. Coupled with an extra regulator, it is worn in addition to regular tanks and is used only in the event someone runs out of air.

Mandatory in cave exploration, and often used by ice divers, a safety reel holding several hundred feet of braided nylon line minimizes the danger of getting lost. Such a rig is a guideline rather than a lifeline. That is, a diver isn't

Underwater lights should have sturdy pressure-resistant cases and a high-quality lens or sealed beam lamp. Lights with wrist loops are easier to carry and less likely to be lost.

hauled to the surface by the safety line but follows it back when visibility is limited or when it is essential that he exit from the exact spot he entered the water.

A buddy line is a length of strong cord, 8 to 10 feet long, which you and your diving partner hold onto to keep from being separated in dirty water or at night. Needless to say, a buddy line is useful only in areas free of obstruction and marine growth.

On a night dive, or on a cave or wreck exploration dive, *each* diver must have a reliable, good-quality underwater light. Satisfactory lights are powered by at least four D-size dry cells, or a 6-volt dry cell, or nickel cadmium batteries. Some lights have sealed beam units, and some have rechargeable batteries. An underwater light must be closed off by a soft rubber gasket and have a completely waterproof switch. (Tip: For a perfect seal, spread lubricating jelly or petrolatum, such as Vaseline, on the gasket before seating it in its channel and screwing on the cover.) To prevent dropping your light underwater, fasten a length of braided nylon cord to the handle and loop it around your wrist. After every dive, rinse the outside of your light in fresh water, dry it, and remove the batteries. Leaking batteries have been known to build up enough pressure to blow a light apart.

Diver Propulsion Vehicles

A diver propulsion vehicle (DPV) for underwater travel looks like a junior-sized torpedo. It has a headlight in the nose and a shielded propeller in the tail, and it operates from a self-contained battery. You don't ride on it but instead grip a pair of control handles and let it pull you through the water at a speed of two or three knots, which is faster than you can swim wearing scuba gear. The DPV is used mostly by professionals who need to cover large sectors of ocean floor.

Floats, Boats, Flags, and Whistles

Even if you wear a buoyancy compensator vest, it's a good idea to have some kind of surface float to rest on or to put game and spear guns on when going to and from a diving area. Probably the simplest and cheapest rig is an inner tube with an attached length of line for tying to kelp or to a rock. As a refinement to this humble float, you can attach a burlap bag to hold shells, fish, lobsters, or other loot.

A commercial surf mat is made of rubber and canvas and looks like an

An underwater propulsion vehicle enables a diver to cover more territory and conserve energy. Even with such mechanical help, buddy teams must be maintained on every dive, so each member should be equipped with his or her own UPV.

air mattress, but, unlike an air mattress, it is built to take rougher use and puncture far less easily. For swimming along on the surface, with a minimum expenditure of energy, lie flat on the mat and use your fins for propulsion. In spite of its name, don't try riding a surf mat through surf when wearing diving gear or you may be dumped and lose some of your equipment.

Sleek fiberglass kayaks made especially for divers let you paddle about swiftly and also serve as a resting platform. They are expensive but efficient.

With any kind of float, you should use a "diver's down" flag to let the world know that you're there. The international diver's flag—rarely seen in the United States—is blue and white. The diver's flag used in this country has a rectangular red field with a diagonal white stripe. Such flags signal that divers are operating in the area. A diver's flag should be mounted at least 30 inches above the water on a shaft secured to a surface float. For your own safety, stay fairly near your flag, ranging no more than 100 feet away. Boat operators are supposed to honor such flags by keeping clear, and most do. However, as a safeguard against your coming up under a churning propeller, don't dive in areas of heavy marine traffic. If there is a motorboat around when you're underwater—and you'll know it by the whine of its propellers—don't surface until it goes away.

At the surface, waving to another diver or toward the shore is a recognized distress signal. However, because such motions are not always seen, many divers depend on a plastic whistle for surface communication, fastening it to their flotation vest with an 8-inch length of line.

BOAT DIVING

More and more divers are diving from inflatable craft or live-aboard vessels. Though boat diving is relatively more costly than shore diving, it eliminates much of the physical exertion associated with the latter. Most of the same skills are used in either boat or shore diving, but certain techniques are unique to certain types of vessels and must be clearly understood.

During formal diver training your instructor will inform you, in advance of your first open-water experience, if you'll be diving from a boat. Aboard, the captain will explain the rules and emergency procedures, show you the diving platform, and describe entry and exit techniques. Any special situations or requirements will be covered. If in doubt about anything, question your instructor.

EQUIPMENT CHECKLIST

Many a diver has arrived at the dive site only to discover that his snorkel or weight belt has been left at home. As a safeguard against such disasters, stow equipment in one place between dives to assure its being available. The day before a dive, make sure all is ready and in good working order. On the way to the dive site, keep your gear in a duffel bag or a rigid container to protect it and to prevent anything from becoming lost.

The following checklist is a reminder that even experienced divers may find handy in making predive preparations.

Basic Equipment
- Duffel bag
- Face mask, with snorkel attached
- Fins
- Flotation vest
- Weight belt
- Exposure suit
- Hood
- Gloves
- Booties
- Air tank (filled), with backpack
- Regulator
- Knife
- Compass
- Depth gauge
- Surface float, with line
- Diver's down flag
- Whistle attached to vest

Supplementary Items
- Underwater light
- Spear gun
- Abalone iron
- Game gauge
- Game bag

Ditty Bag
- Certification card
- Spare "O" rings
- Spare snorkel keeper
- First aid kit
- Fishing license
- Tide tables
- Canteen of water
- Swim suit
- Towel
- Diver's logbook
- Coins for emergency calls
- A copy of this list

A diver's logbook (front) is an up-to-date record of diving experience and underwater time. A training record (rear) is a register of instruction and continuing education, as well as an account of conditions encountered in different geographical locations and diving-related excursions.

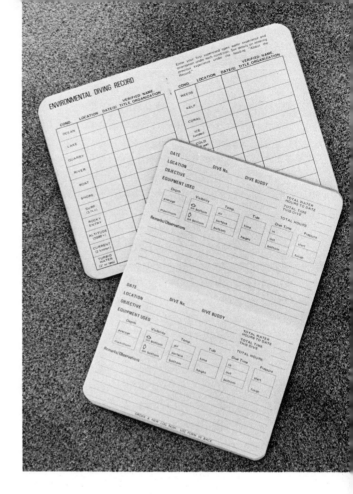

If you plan to make notes underwater—survey information, camera data, or your own thoughts—you can use a smooth plastic slate with an attached grease pencil, or a matte-finish slate and a lead pencil. (Slates are also useful for communication between divers.) And if you're really data conscious, a diver's logbook gives you an organized place to record each dive, with space for jotting observations and comments. Logbooks are becoming increasingly important as a record of one's experience and underwater time.

IF YOU'RE GOING AFTER GAME

As curious and unafraid as fish are—you can actually touch some before they'll move—you cannot catch sizable ones with your bare hands. If you decide to go after moving game underwater, you have several types of spear guns to choose from.

The pole spear (also called hand sling) is a long shaft with a spearhead at one end and a rubber loop at the other. To "load" it, you slip the loop over one wrist and force the butt end of the spear back through that hand, clutching the shaft firmly until you're ready to fire. A Hawaiian sling is a spearheaded shaft that slips into a 3-inch-long wooden barrel with an attached rubber loop. You hold the barrel with one hand, slip the spear shaft into it, engaging the rubber loop, and pull back the spear with the other hand. Using this sling is like shooting an arrow from a bow.

Both the pole spear and the Hawaiian sling are powerful, short-range weapons, but they require considerable practice for accuracy. Gas-powered spears (CO_2 cartridges) are simple to operate and very powerful, but the noise of their blasting off usually frightens away any unspeared fish in the vicinity. Rubber-powered spear guns have a long aluminum barrel, a molded pistol grip with a safety catch, one or more rubber slings, and a spear shaft. They are perhaps the most widely used. A novice should start out with the single-sling model before trying the more powerful versions.

Breakaway spearheads are recommended to keep the shaft from being bent as a speared fish struggles. With any spear gun, use a long shaft for open water and a short shaft in rocky areas to keep from blunting heads that miss. Also with any spear gun, use a lot of common sense. Spear guns are lethal weapons, as potentially dangerous as any other kind of gun. They are made to kill what they're pointed at upon release of the trigger, and they are just as capable of skewering a 200-pound man as they are of killing a 100-pound fish.

Along most of the East and West Coasts, lobster is the prize game. In Caribbean and Gulf waters, various fish are popular. On the northern California coast the abalone—a large mollusk something like a giant clam on the half shell—entices many divers. Abalones are not simply plucked from their home on an underwater rock but must be pried free with a length of flat steel, a tool called an ab iron. An abalone iron should be 12 to 14 inches long and 1 to 2 inches wide and should be tapered to a chisel edge at the business end. It should have a slight bend in it to act as a prying fulcrum. The handle can be wrapped with black tape or have a grip similar to that on a bicycle handlebar. To keep from dropping the ab iron, attach it to your wrist with a loop of surgical tubing.

Because fish and game laws are strictly enforced, an ab iron should have markings on it so you can measure your catch to be sure it's legal size. Better yet is a caliper type of gauge that measures exact outside dimensions, which is what the game warden is interested in and will hold you to if he chooses to inspect your catch.

To hold your underwater harvest, whether it be abalone, lobster, fish,

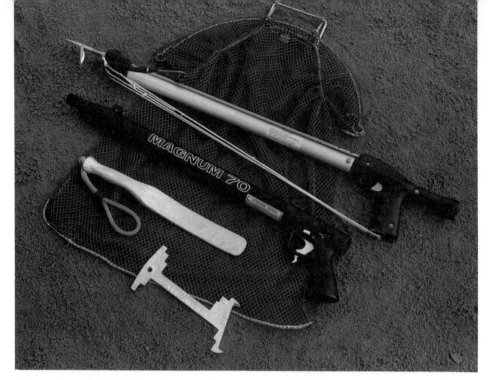

Game-hunting success is more likely with the proper equipment. From bottom: all-purpose tool for measuring lobsters, clams, and abalones; abalone iron with wrist loop; pneumatic spear gun; standard single-band spear gun. Game can be carried in the nylon mesh bag.

shells, or artifacts, you may want to have a canvas or net game bag (also called a goody bag) fastened to your weight belt. A game bag will trail along as you swim, but make sure it doesn't drift around in the water and get snagged on your quick-release buckles.

KEEPING IT ALL TOGETHER

Equipment should be properly cared for after and between dives to ensure its always being ready and in good shape. You can't afford to be lazy about your equipment.

Turn off the tank valve, purge the regulator, and remove it from the tank. Make sure there is no water or dirt in the dust cap before replacing it on the high-pressure seat of the regulator; even a few drops of salt water in the filter may cause deterioration. Carefully blow out the dust cap by holding it close to the tank valve seat and cracking the valve open slightly, then immediately put the cap on the regulator and keep it there. Put a plastic cap (available at dive shops) or a piece of tape over the tank valve seat to keep it clean and to prevent loss of the "O" ring. When you remove the tape from the valve seat, make sure the "O" ring isn't sticking to it.

Rinse every piece of gear thoroughly with fresh water, drain, and let dry in open air but not direct sun. Rinsing is advised after a nonsaltwater dive too, because even the clearest of lakes, rivers, or ponds have some suspended particles or silt, which will shorten equipment life or clog moving parts.

Store protective suits on large hangers in a cool, dark closet. Folding or rolling them causes creases, which become points of deterioration. A buoyancy compensator vest should have a little air in it to prevent wrinkling and to keep

Dive bags help keep equipment together on the beach or in a boat, and after a dive wet gear can be contained for transporting. Every piece of diving equipment should be clearly marked with the owner's name.

the insides from sticking together. Keep delicate items—regulator, face mask, depth gauge, compass—separate from weights, knives, or ab irons to prevent damage.

Periodically lubricate zippers with a light application of silicone spray. Never use oil or grease on valves, regulators, or any other part of your breathing gear because they are harmful to the lungs, and oil combined with oxygen may explode in high-pressure air.

For transporting your equipment, use a sturdy duffel bag or a large plastic garbage can. Pack and repack the same way every time so you'll know where to find each item. It's a good idea to pack in the reverse order that you'll be donning the equipment so that, when you take something out, you'll put it on instead of laying it down and perhaps forgetting it. Because the weight belt is the last item to put on, it will always be at the bottom, which helps make the container stable and easy to handle.

In a separate ditty bag you might keep small extras, such as a first-aid kit, spare "O" rings for the high-pressure seat of your tank valve (if you don't have an "O" ring on your first stage, you don't have a dive), decongestant tablets, a jar of honey for energy, a canteen of water.

An all-purpose container, or else a ditty bag, contains such items as spare "O" rings, an extra fin strap, patching material, coins for the telephone, and sunblock lotion. Over time you will develop your own collection of emergency supplies.

The wreck of *Rocas,* in the British Virgin Islands, is but one of many such sites that can be explored in relatively shallow waters.

Matter, Motion, and You

Underwater Physics and Physiology

Every day people examine the world around them a little more carefully, become a little more aware of their natural surroundings. The realization that the earth, its waters, and its atmosphere are not limitless has given them a fresh appreciation for the value of their world, and they have set out to learn more about how they can live in harmony with it. The necessity for clean air and clear water is especially driven home when people climb high into the upper altitudes or dive deep into the ocean.

Because both environments are alien to human beings, however, they must make certain bodily adjustments when they enter them. Fortunately, the human body is a remarkably efficient machine. It can withstand considerable change in pressure and temperature; it can convert oxygen and nourishment into energy to fuel its vital functions; it can regenerate living cells to combat illness and injury. Yet, with all of this adaptability, and despite their determination to extend themselves, human beings are bound by certain unalterable physical limitations. Let's take a look at some of the conditions that human divers meet in the underwater world.

71

PHYSICAL PROPERTIES UNDERWATER

We carry out our daily existence submerged in a sea of air, immersed in an ocean of atmosphere. Living from birth in this surrounding, we are used to breathing a certain mixture of gases at certain pressures. We are accustomed to moving our bodies through a medium of certain density, usually in an upright position. When we enter the denser underwater world, all the physical properties we are familiar with—sound, light, heat, our own weight—change drastically. Some of the changes can be startling the first time they are experienced. Some of the differences can be unsettling, even dangerous, unless we have an appreciation of what is happening to us and know how to react to it.

Buoyancy

One of the most pronounced changes we notice on submerging in water for the first time is relative weightlessness, the feeling of being pushed upward. In simple terms, buoyancy is the tendency for an object to float on the surface of a liquid. Another way to put this is that the liquid has the power to keep an object from sinking. This familiar yet fascinating property is expressed by Archimedes' Principle, which says that any object wholly or partially immersed in a liquid is buoyed up by a force equal to the weight of the liquid displaced.

One cubic foot of salt water weighs 64 pounds. If you were to completely submerge an object that displaced a cubic foot of water, that object would in effect weigh 64 pounds less in salt water than it would on dry land, regardless of the weight or shape of the object.

Let's assume that a fully dressed scuba diver weighing, say, 186 pounds displaces 3 cubic feet of water, or 192 pounds ($3 \times 64 = 192$). Subtracting the diver's weight of 186 pounds from the weight of water displaced, 192 pounds, we find a difference of 6 pounds. Because the diver displaces a volume of water that weighs more than his body weight, he will have what is known as a positive buoyancy, amounting to 6 pounds. That is, he will be light and will tend to float. For comfortable diving he will have to add at least 6 pounds of weight to achieve neutral buoyancy, the point at which he effectively weighs nothing and moves underwater with greatest ease. The addition of more weight than that will give him negative buoyancy; he will be heavy and will tend to sink.

Two points should be remembered concerning buoyancy:

1. A skin diver who is neutral at the surface will become negatively buoyant at about 20 feet as his lungs become compressed with depth. To the sport diver, who seldom goes much deeper, this amount of negative buoyancy will be insignificant and won't hinder his return to the surface.

2. A diver wearing scuba and a wet suit has air bubbles trapped between suit and body as well as in the cells of the suit. As he descends, the bubbles will be compressed and he will become negatively buoyant at about 20 to 30 feet. The deeper he goes, the more negative he will become. One indication will be an apparent loosening of his weight belt as the wet suit is squashed against his body with increasing pressure. (For this reason, weight belts should be worn snug.) Putting a breath or two into his buoyancy compensator vest will offset the negative tendencies and bring him back to a neutral condition.

HOW TO DETERMINE YOUR BUOYANCY

When neutrally buoyant you neither sink nor float, and underwater movement is achieved with minimum effort. As a rough guide, you'll have to wear one pound of belt weight for every ten pounds of body weight for neutral buoyancy. However, there are no all-purpose formulas for computing exact buoyancy because no two persons have exactly the same body weight, dimensions, or bone structure. The only way to go about it is to get in the water wearing everything you'll have on when you dive.

Enter the deep end of a swimming pool fully dressed in diving gear. Start with weights on your belt amounting to 10 to 12 percent of your body weight. Gradually add or subtract weights until you can maintain an underwater swimming position without exertion. You are then weighted properly for fresh-water diving.

Salt water, being denser than fresh water, necessitates adding a bit more weight. Begin as above in the swimming pool and add weight until you're just lying on the bottom of the pool without really trying to stay down. When you take a deep breath on scuba, your chest should barely rise off the bottom, and on exhaling you should sink and feel slightly heavy on the bottom. Providing that you wear the same equipment and use the same size tank in the ocean, you should find yourself neutrally buoyant at the start of your dive.

Remember that the deeper you dive, the more negatively buoyant you'll become. If you feel yourself sinking at about 30 feet, put a puff or two of air in your personal flotation vest in order to make yourself lighter.

Sound Transmission

Sound travels through water nearly four times as fast as it does in air: 4,800 feet per second in water; 1,090 feet per second in air. Generally speaking, this is because a more dense medium is a better conductor of sound waves.

Despite the superior sound transmission qualities of water, divers cannot communicate verbally without some mechanical assistance because most of the sound energy underwater is scattered and absorbed before it can travel more than a few inches. Underwater communication systems are used effectively by military and scientific teams, but such equipment at present is beyond the needs and financial means of most sport divers.

If you need to attract attention underwater, you can tap on your tank with your knife or a rock. Such sounds can be heard clearly at some distance. However, if visibility is poor, the point of origin of the sound will be difficult for another diver to locate because of water's scattering characteristics.

Light and Visibility

The human eye has evolved its function of seeing in air, a very thin medium. Water, being much more dense, scatters (diffracts) light rays to such a degree that the bare eye in contact with it can discern light and dark but cannot make out shapes and details well. It takes a captive bubble of air in front of the eyes—the function of the face mask—to redirect the image-carrying light rays and restore clear vision.

With a face mask, vision may be good underwater, but it is still not quite the same as in air. In addition to diffracting light rays, water refracts (bends) them because it actually makes them travel slower. The result is a distortion that causes everything underwater to appear closer and larger than it actually is. This takes some getting used to when you reach for an object, such as a shell, or try to spear a fish.

Water also absorbs light and decreases general illumination. Nearly three-fourths of all light rays penetrating water are absorbed and diffused by suspended particles within 20 feet of the light source. Rough seas and a stirred-up bottom can reduce penetration even more.

Colors differ in how they are absorbed by water. Red is clearly discernible to a depth of only 10 to 20 feet, after which it appears to turn gray. Orange and yellow fade out at 30 to 40 feet. Cool colors, such as blue and green, retain

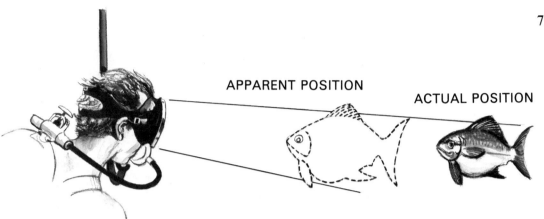

APPARENT POSITION

ACTUAL POSITION

Refraction. An object viewed through a face mask appears closer and larger than it actually is. This distortion, called refraction, is caused by the bending of light rays as they pass through a dense medium—water—and then a less dense medium—the air trapped in front of your eyes.

their hues to below 100 feet; this is one reason blue predominates as a color for wet suits. Divers interested in underwater photography would do well to read one or more of the many good books on the subject.

Heat and Cold

Perhaps the greatest limitation to diving is water temperature. If you're uncomfortably cold, you're not going to enjoy yourself no matter how much there is to see or do. A swimming pool may feel warm when you stick your hand into it, but when you are submerged for a while the water is going to drain heat from your body. This is because water is a poor insulator and a good thermal conductor. If body temperature is allowed to remain even a few degrees below normal for long, cramps and loss of coordination may result.

The wearing of protective suits helps conserve body heat and delay the onset of chills. The wise diver will always terminate a dive before becoming incapacitated by shivering, muscle cramps, and numbness.

A good reserve of body heat can be ensured by proper eating and drinking habits. The body is an engine that runs on fuel (food and fluids) and creates energy (heat). Nourishing it insufficiently or improperly will deprive it of its fuel and decrease its output. Though eating heavily prior to entering the water is unwise, a hearty, high-carbohydrate meal at the beginning of a diving day and a high-protein meal at its end will replenish energy losses. Often a candy bar or a tablespoon of honey just before a dive helps stoke the engine with calories for heat energy.

Alcohol in the system acts as a stimulant initially, but, as mentioned in Chapter 2, it becomes a depressant as the initial effects wear off. In addition, the immediate warmth achieved from drinking is a false indication. Alcohol has a diuretic effect—it increases the flow of urine—which causes the loss of body heat and also dehydration. Alcohol also slows down blood circulation. Chilling results, and the body becomes susceptible to more serious maladies. Because the effects of alcohol are so varied, the wisest rule is to not drink the night before a dive.

THE AIR YOU BREATHE

The dictionary defines atmosphere as the body of gases surrounding the earth. More simply, atmosphere is the air you breathe.

The air you breathe is not one gas but a mixture of several gases. Nowadays, some of these are man-made (smog), but most exist as the natural state of the atmosphere. Three of these gases—oxygen, nitrogen, and carbon dioxide—are of special interest to the diver.

Oxygen is the only gas capable of supporting life by itself. Even so, it accounts for only approximately 21 percent of the atmosphere in terms of volume. Oxygen is colorless, tasteless, and odorless except in high concentrations. Despite its life-sustaining qualities, oxygen has a poisonous effect on the body under high pressure.

Nitrogen makes up approximately 79 percent of the atmosphere, or four-fifths of its volume. Nitrogen too is colorless, tasteless, and odorless. It is incapable of supporting life by itself. Under high concentrations nitrogen has an intoxicating effect on the body, a phenomenon commonly known as nitrogen narcosis.

The smallest gas by volume in air—.03 percent—but one of the most important, carbon dioxide is a by-product of respiration. Interestingly, it is the gas responsible for triggering the breathing process. Carbon dioxide is colorless, odorless, and tasteless in normal concentrations. In high concentrations it has an acid taste and a sharp odor. An excess of carbon dioxide in the body can cause severe headache or, at worst, suffocation.

Though air contains small amounts of other gases, the only one of importance to you as a sport diver is carbon monoxide, which is colorless, odorless, and tasteless, but highly poisonous. Carbon monoxide results from incomplete combustion of carbon fuels such as gasoline. If it contaminates a diver's air supply, it can cause fainting and death of body tissue.

An unknown wreck at a depth of 15 feet off St. Thomas, American Virgin Islands, entices a free diver.

YOUR BREATHING NEEDS

A healthy body can normally keep its cells supplied with sufficient oxygen to sustain life even when it is working strenuously, and it can produce enough carbon dioxide to maintain normal respiratory functions. There are times when a diver needs to know the amount of oxygen he is consuming, how much carbon dioxide he is producing, or how much air he requires for certain depths. The following figures, compiled by the U.S. Navy, will give you some idea of these respiratory needs. Note that as exertion increases, so do respiratory needs.

Oxygen Consumption on Land

Activity	Pints per minute
Rest: Basal	0.5
Rest: Standing still	0.8
Light work: Walking, 2 mph	1.4
Moderate work: Walking, 4 mph	2.4
Heavy work: Swimming, 1 knot	3.6
Severe work: Running, 8 mph	4.0
Severe work: Running uphill	8.0

(Adapted from U.S. Navy Diving Manual, 1970)

The following table shows that under normal diving conditions the average scuba diver consumes air at the rate of about three pints per minute. Because body metabolism varies considerably from person to person, these oxygen consumption figures should be taken only as a general guide.

Oxygen Consumption for Swimmers

Activity	Pints per minute
Rest: On bottom	0.6
Light work: Scuba, .5 knot	1.6
Moderate work: Average scuba, .85 knot	2.8
Heavy work: Fast scuba, 1 knot	3.6
Severe work: Swimming all out, 1.2 knots	5.0

(Adapted from U.S. Navy Diving Manual, 1970)

What's the point of all these statistics? Well, as Dr. Christopher W. Dueker, U.S.N., points out in his book, *Medical Aspects of Sport Diving*, the wide range of oxygen consumption for various human activities, from 0.6 pint at rest to 5 pints for hard swimming, illustrates vividly that swimming is an inefficient means of propulsion. Two pints of oxygen will suffice for a 116-yard run at 8 mph, but the same amount is good for only 14 yards of 1-knot swimming. This means that, in order to make the very best use of available air, divers must perfect techniques for moving with the least possible effort and for breathing with the greatest possible ease.

Oxygen Debt

Our ability to work as divers is directly dependent on the maximum usage capacity of our heart and lungs. This is our normal working load. However, the body has an interesting built-in safety valve known as oxygen debt. The body can work under extreme conditions for a short period of time with less than the normal body requirement of oxygen, a phenomenon that has saved the life of more than one diver. The oxygen that is "owed" to the body must be repaid soon, however. The capacity of each person's oxygen debt is proportional to his or her level of physical fitness. A diver in good condition can sustain a greater oxygen debt capacity than one who is out of shape and so can sustain himself longer in an emergency.

Capacity of the Lungs

Human beings breathe mainly to supply their cells with oxygen and to flush excess, metabolically created carbon dioxide out of the system. The breathing or respiratory cycle involves inhalation, rest, and exhalation. During a normal respiratory cycle the amount of air moved in and out of the lungs is four to five pints; this is known as tidal volume. Tidal volume may increase during exertion, but it will never exceed vital capacity. Vital capacity is the greatest volume of air a person can expel from the lungs after a full breath. Average vital capacity is around eight pints, which is about 80 percent of the maximum lung capacity.

WHAT IS PRESSURE?

Of all the physical influences on a diver, pressure is perhaps the most strongly felt. Understanding pressure can make your diving more pleasurable and can help you avoid accidents. But what is pressure?

A gas is composed of molecules that are in constant motion, bouncing off one another and colliding with any solid surface in the vicinity, whether it be water, a tree, or you. The force of these collisions is measured as pressure.

As you sit reading this book, you aren't aware of atmospheric pressure because it is exerted on you equally from all directions and because you have been subjected to it from birth. When you dive beneath the surface of a body of water, however, you feel a difference because in addition to atmospheric pressure pressing down on the water and on you, your body is pressed upon by an added weight—a pressure—of water.

Atmospheric Pressure

The pressure of air around us, called atmospheric pressure, exerts a constant 14.7 pounds per square inch (psi). If you had a cylinder with a cross-section of 1 square inch extending from sea level to the upper limits of the atmosphere, the air it contained would weigh 14.7 pounds. This weight of 14.7 psi is known as one atmosphere of pressure, and it is a figure that you will encounter often in diving.

Because water is the medium surrounding a diver, let's look at pressure another way. One cubic foot of salt water weighs 64 pounds (fresh water, being less dense, weighs 62.4 pounds per cubic foot). If we were to take a cubic foot of salt water and multiply the height, 12 inches, by the width, 12 inches, by the depth, 12 inches, we would have a total of 1,728 cubic inches. Dividing the weight of a cubic foot of salt water by 1,728, we obtain .0371 pound as the weight of 1 cubic inch of sea water. Multiplying by 12 (12 $\times$ .0371) gives the pressure of a 1-inch square column of sea water 12 inches deep as .445 pound. Now multiply the number of feet of any depth by .445 to find the pressure for that depth. As a rule of thumb, pressure increases .5 pound for every foot of descent.

For example, at 10 feet the pressure is 10 $\times$ .445, or 4.45 psi. At 20 feet it is 8.90 psi. And at 33 feet it is 14.7 psi, the same as atmospheric pressure. Thus, for every 33 feet of depth, pressure increases by 14.7 psi, or 1 atmosphere.

Absolute Pressure

Every time a diver goes below the surface he is subjected to the surface pressure (atmospheric) pushing down on the water, plus the water pressure (ambient); the total of the two is called absolute pressure. Any time that pressure is computed for any depth, the formula .445 × feet of depth + 14.7 gives absolute pressure. For example, the following table computes pressure for four depths.

Depth	Computation
At 33 feet:	.445 × 33 feet = 14.7
	plus <u>14.7</u>
	29.4 psi, which is 2 atmospheres absolute
At 66 feet:	.445 × 66 feet = 29.4
	plus <u>14.7</u>
	44.1 psi, or 3 atmospheres absolute
At 99 feet:	.445 × 99 feet = 44.1
	plus <u>14.7</u>
	58.8 psi, or 4 atmospheres absolute
At 132 feet:	.445 × 132 feet = 58.8
	plus <u>14.7</u>
	73.5 psi, or 5 atmospheres absolute

When answers to diving problems are calculated, pressure is always figured in terms of absolute pressure.

Gauge Pressure

Pressures are usually measured with gauges that read zero at sea level. Gauges indicate the actual pressure being measured, not atmospheric pressure, and their readings are in pounds per square inch gauge (psig). Remember that your diving tank gauge reads the pressure of the air inside the tank, not the pressure of the water on your body.

THE BEHAVIOR OF GASES

When a volume of gas is subjected to increasing pressure, gas molecules are brought into closer contact. To understand more fully how important this is

Up from the bottom, a diver brings a pair of starfish, which thrive from tide line to depths well over 100 feet.

in diving, let's see how the gases that make up our breathing medium are affected by pressure. Four gas laws are very important to compressed air diving.

Boyle's Law

Boyle's Law explains how underwater pressure causes changes in the volume of gas in your lungs as you change depth. The law states that with temperature constant, the volume of a gas varies inversely with absolute pressure, and its density varies directly. This means simply that when pressure on a gas increases, the volume of the gas shrinks and the density of the gas becomes greater.

For example, if the pressure on a gas is doubled, as it is at 33 feet beneath the surface, the density of the gas is also doubled but its volume is decreased by half. This effect is known as Boyle's Law, and it is very important to you as a diver because it says that the deeper you go, the less time you're going to be able to stay there.

If a diver descends to 66 feet, the density of his self-contained air supply is tripled and its volume is cut to one-third. At 132 feet the density is five times as great and the volume is one-fifth the original volume.

If a balloon containing 100 pints of air at the surface were taken down to 33 feet, its volume would be compressed by half, to 50 pints. Further descent to 66 feet would reduce the volume to one-third the original amount, or 33.3 pints. Thus the actual change becomes smaller and smaller with increasing depth. The greatest pressure changes take place near the surface.

Now, if an empty balloon were filled to a volume of 33.3 pints of air at 66 feet below the surface and brought up, the volume would expand to 100 pints at the surface. And if you were to take a deep breath at, say, 33 feet down and then ascend while holding that breath, the air in your lungs would also expand with decreasing water pressure. By the time you reached the surface, the captive air in your lungs would have doubled in volume; it would have been driven into your chest cavity or chest tissues, causing severe damage or possibly death.

The following table gives the effects of Boyle's Law for scuba divers.

Atmospheric Pressure (Absolute)	psi	Depth in Feet	Usable Tank Volume	Approximate Time to Breath Tank*
1 (atmosphere)	14.7	0	Full	60 min.
2	29.4	33	1/2	30 min.
3	44.1	66	1/3	20 min.
4	58.8	99	1/4	15 min.
5	73.5	132	1/5	12 min.
6	88.2	165	1/6	10 min.

*Based on a breathing rate of 60 min. at atm. pressure.

with a half-full tank (36 cubic feet, 1,125 psi), his effective breathing time at 33 feet would be only about 18 minutes. For safety's sake, always begin a dive with a full tank. You never know when you'll need all the air you can get.

Dalton's Law

In any mixture of gases, each gas exerts a proportionate share of the total pressure being produced. Dalton's Law states that the total pressure exerted by a gaseous mixture is the sum of the pressures that would be exerted by each of the gases if it alone were present and occupied the total volume.

Remember that air is a gas made up of approximately 80 percent nitrogen and 20 percent oxygen, and remember that in diving we are dealing with a total pressure at the surface of 14.7 psi. The partial pressure of each component of air becomes increasingly important to a diver the deeper he goes. As an example, at sea level the partial pressure of nitrogen, being almost 80 percent of the whole, is $14.7 \times .80 = 11.76$ psi, and the partial pressure of oxygen (about 20 percent of the whole) is $14.7 \times .20 = 2.94$ psi.

At 33 feet, absolute pressure is doubled, so the partial pressure of nitrogen would be 23.4 psi and that of oxygen, 5.88 psi. At 132 feet, or five atmospheres, which is the recommended limit for sport divers, the partial pressure of nitrogen is 58.5 psi and that of oxygen, 14.7 psi. The partial pressure of a gas may be unimportant at the surface, since we are used to living at 1 atmosphere, but increasing gas pressure causes certain physiological changes that can affect your bodily functions.

The following table shows partial pressures of gases at varying depth.

Atmospheres	Depth in Feet	Oxygen	Partial Pressure	Nitrogen
1	0	20%	2.94 p.s.i.	80% 11.76 p.s.i.
2	33	20%	5.88 p.s.i.	80% 23.52 p.s.i.
3	66	20%	8.82 p.s.i.	80% 35.28 p.s.i.
4	99	20%	11.76 p.s.i.	80% 47.04 p.s.i.
5	132	20%	14.7 p.s.i.	80% 58.80 p.s.i.

Based on an air supply relationship of 20% oxygen, 80% nitrogen

Henry's Law

Henry's Law deals with gases under pressure being driven into solution in a liquid, a phenomenon of interest to you as a diver, since the liquid is your blood and the deeper you dive the more nitrogen becomes dissolved in it. At a constant temperature, the amount of gas that will be forced into solution in a liquid is directly proportional to the partial pressure of the gas.

Under pressure, the components of air go into solution in the blood and in body tissues. Because nitrogen is the greatest component of air, it will be absorbed at a rate of four to one over oxygen. The actual rate of solubilities will vary with individuals, owing to absorption differences in fatty and water tissues. These differences partially explain why some divers are affected by nitrogen narcosis and other diving diseases sooner than others.

Gas molecules will dissolve in the blood and tissues until they reach equilibrium with the absolute pressure. However, this process takes time, and so does the reverse process of ridding the body of excess gas molecules. If a diver who has had components of air dissolved in his system ascends faster than the gases can come out of solution, they are going to cause trouble.

Charles's Law, or Gay-Lussac's Law

A final gas law that applies to the diver in a different way is Charles's Law, which states that the volume of a gas varies directly with temperature. This law applies chiefly to the filling of diving cylinders and the handling of inflatable floats and surf mats.

Rising temperatures will increase pressure at the rate of 5 psi for each degree increase. Thus, a diving cylinder filled to 2,000 pounds at 70°F. will have 2,200 pounds at 110°F. and 2,350 pounds at 140°F. This is important to the diver who plans a dive according to the gauge pressure of the tank: once diver and tank hit water that is colder than the surrounding air, the tank pressure is going to drop. For an accurate reading, the submersible pressure gauge should be double-checked when the cylinder is submerged and its temperature is equal to that of the water. Tanks should not be filled to extreme pressure, which creates heat that in turn may cause structural strain. For the same reason, full tanks and surf mats shouldn't be left lying in the sun.

PRESSURE EFFECTS ON DESCENT

Your body is capable of adapting to considerable differences in pressure without physical damage because it is composed chiefly of liquids and solids, both of which are incompressible. However, your body also contains certain hollow spaces, and these must at all times have free access to air. When a differential of pressure occurs over these spaces, discomfort or pain occurs. An injury resulting from pressure differences, whether during descent or ascent, is called barotrauma.

Ears, Sinuses, and Teeth

The sinuses are air-filled cavities in the skull above and behind the nose. They are connected by hollow passages to the nasal cavity. If these passages are blocked, as by unnatural growth or mucous drainage, air will not be able to move freely from the sinuses, and any increase in external pressure will put

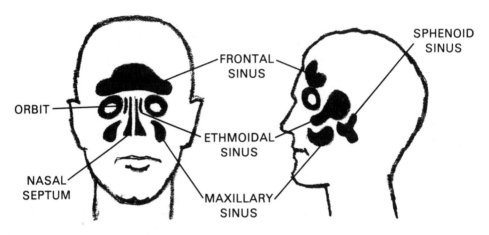

Sinuses are air-filled cavities in the bones of the skull, connecting with the nasal cavity. If any of these air pockets are blocked when external pressure increases (as during descent underwater), pain will be felt over the eyes, in the upper reaches of the nose, or in the upper jaw. When a diver is suffering from any kind of congestion, he should stay out of the water.

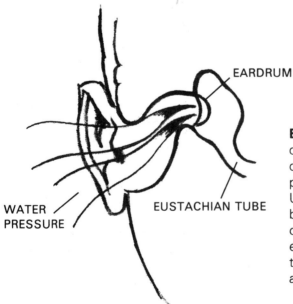

Ear squeeze, one of the most common diving disorders, is caused by water pressure pushing against the eardrum. Unless this external pressure is balanced, or equalized, by a counterpressure behind the eardrum, the eardrum's flexible tissue will be painfully distorted and may rupture.

pressure on them that cannot be relieved. This is referred to as sinus squeeze. Air in the middle ear, behind the eardrum, is normally free to move through the Eustachian tube to the throat. If the Eustachian tube is obstructed and pressure is applied to the outer ear, the trapped air cannot move and the tympanic membrane, or eardrum, will be distorted inward, with resulting pain. This is called ear squeeze. Squeeze usually occurs at depths anywhere from 5 to 15 feet. To descend beyond the point of pain without doing something about it may cause severe damage that will need medical attention.

The most serious injury is rupturing an eardrum in water several degrees below body temperature. Cold water rushing into the middle ear will upset your equilibrium, resulting in vertigo and nausea. If this happens, keep calm and don't try to surface until your orientation returns, which will happen as soon as the water in your ear has warmed to body temperature. Upon surfacing, you may have some bleeding and drainage, accompanied by additional pain and disorientation. Don't put anything in your ear, but see a doctor right away because blood in the ear is a prime culture for infection. Through prompt and proper medical care, healing will take only a few weeks. Even after a perforated eardrum has mended, don't dive until your doctor gives you an okay.

Earplugs should *never* be worn by divers. Pressure at only a few feet of depth will drive them deep into the ears, trapping air outside the eardrum and making equalization impossible.

Tooth squeeze is caused by a tiny amount of trapped air in a tooth or by a microscopic crack, and equalizing will do little to relieve localized discomfort in the teeth. If the squeeze is minor enough, you can try to ignore it; if it's really painful, you'll just have to scrub the dive. Tooth squeeze may require you to replace a previous filling.

Lung Squeeze

As a scuba diver descends, breathing compressed air from his tank, pressure in his lungs matches absolute pressure, and the lungs and thoracic region remain in equilibrium. However, in free diving—skin diving—no high-pressure air is available to the lungs, and increasing absolute pressure will squeeze them. Remember Boyle's Law?

If a skin diver were to start a dive with about 12 pints of air in his lungs and descend to 100 feet, he would have that air compressed to one-fourth its original volume, or 3 pints. This approximates residual volume—the air left in the lungs at sea level after a forced exhalation.

Controlled breath-holding dives to 240 feet have indicated that quantities of blood apparently move through elastic blood vessels into the chest cavity, displacing air and thus decreasing residual volume and offsetting lung squeeze. However, such deep dives are best left to research projects and scientific studies. For a beginning diver, a good rule of thumb is never to dive deeper than a third to a half of the distance you can swim underwater horizontally on a single breath.

Generally, the symptoms of severe lung squeeze are chest pains during descent and difficulty of breath control on return to the surface. First aid for a lung-squeeze victim involves clearing his mouth of foreign matter, giving artificial respiration and oxygen if needed, treating for shock, and summoning a doctor.

Mask Squeeze

Mask squeeze puts pressure against the face and can cause tiny veins in the eyes to rupture. Blowing air through the nose balances external pressure and prevents mask squeeze damage.

Working to Breathe

If breathing at depth seems difficult to you, it's because the density of a given volume of air increases in direct proportion to the depth, or to absolute pressure, even though the volume and breathing rate remain the same. As an example, at 66 feet (three atmospheres) the air you breathe is three times as dense as at the surface, and at 132 feet (five atmospheres) the air is five times as dense. No wonder dragging it into the lungs is labor. The work involved in moving dense air through a regulator and into the respiratory passage reduces your overall ability to work during deep dives.

Poorly designed valves and regulators, or makeshift adaptations, can interfere with relaxed, comfortable breathing. A dry, raspy feeling in the throat generally indicates that considerable effort was made to acquire a lungful of air. If you feel such symptoms, check your equipment to make sure it is in good working order.

Nitrogen Narcosis

Nitrogen makes up nearly 80 percent of the air we breathe. Therefore, every breath contains four-fifths nitrogen, a significant amount considering that this gas, under pressure, has the same effect on the body as certain types of anesthetic gases have. When the partial pressure of nitrogen is increased about fourfold, which occurs at a depth of about 100 feet, body tissues start to become saturated with the gas and the diver experiences a sense of dreaminess, a feeling of intoxication. Though the principle involved is not entirely clear to scientists, it is sometimes referred to as Martini's Law because for every additional 50 feet of depth the effect is equivalent to one martini made with a very good quality of gin. The following effects have been noted as depth is increased:

Physiological Effects of Nitrogen

Depth	*Effect*
Below 100 feet	Lightheadedness, overconfidence, a false feeling of well-being, loss of judgment
Below 150 feet	Merriment, a tendency to talkativeness, dizziness, disorientation
Below 200 feet	Uncontrolled laughter, loss of concentration, delayed responses
Below 250 feet	Muddled thinking, depression, poor coordination
Below 300 feet	Near-unconsciousness

There is some evidence that a person who can build up a tolerance to alcohol can likewise increase resistance to narcosis, but it should be remembered that the depth at which nitrogen narcosis sets in varies considerably with individuals. Some divers may descend to more than 150 feet with absolutely no effects, whereas others may be narked out of their heads at 100 feet. With novice divers, anxiety seems to bring on symptoms sooner, whereas experienced divers can often function safely at depths well beyond the usual scuba sport diving limit of 130 feet, undoubtedly a result of conditioning through numerous deep dives. Nitrogen narcosis dulls the perception to such an extent that the buddy system becomes ineffective, especially if both divers are influenced.

The prevention of narcosis is simple. Don't dive deep! Just about everything of interest can be found above 100 feet. Coral beds don't grow much deeper; kelp forests are found only in shallow water; game hunting is not practical at depths because of the enormous consumption of air in hard swimming. Even photography is impractical, since the deeper you go, the less natural light there is.

When diving anywhere near 100 feet, keep close watch on your buddy.

At the first sign of irrational behavior or recklessness, signal an ascent and surface, or else go up partway and wait until the symptoms disappear.

REVERSE PRESSURE EFFECTS ON ASCENT

The most important physiological effects of increasing pressure during descent are various forms of squeeze. Though such disorders are relatively easy to avoid, they are not to be taken lightly by the conscientious diver. Of even greater importance are certain diving maladies that can occur on ascent or that result from deep diving.

Reverse block is rare but it may result from the Eustachian tubes' becoming plugged with mucus forced into the middle ear during descent. As absolute pressure is reduced during ascent, trapped air within the middle ear will expand, causing the tympanic membrane to distend outward. If the expanding air is not allowed to escape through the Eustachian tube, the eardrum may rupture out. A diver who feels ear pressure during ascent can prevent a rupture by stopping, descending a few feet slowly, then ascending slowly, sucking down against the roof of the mouth while holding the nose. To prevent reverse blocks and trapped air spaces, never dive with a head cold.

Reverse sinus squeeze may occur without your even being aware of it. If on surfacing you discover a little blood in your mask, don't blow your nose hard. Just rinse your mask and face and on subsequent dives that day take more time to equalize pressures when descending and ascending.

Gas may be trapped in the stomach when a diver swallows to clear his throat or to get rid of a mouthful of water. Intestinal gas comes from eating potent foods. On ascent, expanding gastric gases can cause abdominal pains or cramps, but leveling off and expelling them will give relief.

Air Embolism

A very serious diving hazard is air embolism, a bubble in the bloodstream that may block circulation and cause paralysis or death. You can bring about an air embolism by merely holding your breath on ascent after breathing compressed air, so be very careful never to do so.

If a scuba diver holds his breath while coming up from 100 feet, the air in his lungs will expand four times, according to Boyle's Law. In more practical terms, if a diver with 12 pints of air in his lungs ascends from only 33 feet while holding his breath, the air will expand to 24 pints by the time he reaches the surface, a volume far greater than the capacity of the lungs. If the expanding

air isn't allowed to escape, pressure in the lungs becomes greater than the pressure surrounding the chest area, and the tiny air cells in the lungs—the alveoli—will burst, forcing air into the bloodstream, where it may be carried into the brain. An air bubble too large to pass through an artery will become stuck, creating an embolus and halting the passage of blood in that vessel. Starved of an adequate blood supply, the tissues behind the blockage will be quickly damaged.

Although air embolism most often results from intentional breath-holding during ascent, fright or panic may cause a throat spasm to seal off the air passage. Bronchial obstructions such as scars, cysts, and mucus caused by asthma have been reported but are fortunately rare.

Symptoms of an air embolism are bloody sputum, dizziness, disorientation, numbness in arms and legs, convulsions, and cessation of breathing.

Swimming ascents have been made without incident from below 200 feet without breathing gear, but there have also been fatalities while coming up from the bottom of a swimming pool. A hard-and-fast rule is: *When using scuba, always breathe normally and continuously, and never hold your breath.* It doesn't take much of a change in depth to cause a change in pressure, especially near the surface. The last 10 feet are the most critical because it's there that a diver, feeling that he's home free, may tend to hurry up and may forget to exhale.

The technique needed to ascend safely when you have run out of air is covered in Chapter 6.

Mediastinal Emphysema

Mediastinal emphysema refers to air forced into mid-chest tissues. It may be present with an air embolism or may occur separately. Increasing internal lung pressure may cause air from ruptured alveoli to pass along the outside of the blood vessels and bronchi to reach the mediastinum, a space in the middle of the chest. When the air expands in this region with decreasing absolute pressure, it presses against the heart, directly beneath the breastbone. Considerable pain will be felt in the shoulders and arms, and breathing will become very difficult.

Subcutaneous Emphysema

The presence of air under the skin, generally in the throat region, indicates that bubbles have migrated from the mediastinum up to the base of the neck.

Fearless fish accept a fearless diver. Surrounding their visitor, perch press close for an eye-to-eye inspection.

Swelling may occur around the neck, affecting the voice and causing difficulty in swallowing. Unpleasant crackling sounds may be heard from the neck region.

Pneumothorax

An infrequent but serious complication that may arise from overexpansion of air in the alveoli is leakage of air into the pleural cavity, the area between the lungs and the lining of the chest wall. With continuing ascent this trapped air will expand, possibly collapsing a lung and forcing it toward the heart. The symptoms of pneumothorax are sharp chest pains and difficulty in breathing.

Pneumothorax can result from heavy overbreathing under pressure, especially in individuals who have weak spots on the lungs resulting from previous illnesses such as pneumonia or tuberculosis. Smoking can cause pockets of weak lung tissue that will not equalize properly on ascent. Individuals who work at sedentary jobs and have not fully utilized their potential lung capacity are good candidates for pneumothorax, sometimes called "out-of-condition disease."

Treating Ascent Illnesses

The general public can be of little help in dealing with most ascent maladies, since basic first aid does not include treatment of these serious conditions.

Although the chances are slim, the only hope a victim of air embolism has is in immediate recompression (returning to increased pressure) in a recompression chamber. A delay of but two minutes may prove fatal.

If mediastinal or subcutaneous emphysema is not too serious, rest and general medical attention will suffice. Only in the event of great breathing difficulty will recompression be necessary. If pneumothorax is present without air embolism, a doctor may elect to remove the trapped air with a long, hollow needle, and surgery may be necessary to repair lung damage. A recompression chamber would give but temporary relief and is recommended only in conjunction with an air embolism.

DECOMPRESSION SICKNESS

Perhaps the worst diving malady is decompression sickness, referred to as the bends. Although the number of fatalities resulting from the bends is not as great as from air embolism or even nitrogen narcosis, the aftereffects can cripple a diver for the rest of his life. Decompression sickness is a result of decompressing (surfacing) too rapidly, causing nitrogen in the blood and tissues to come out of solution in the form of bubbles.

When a diver ascends directly to the surface after a long and deep dive, the nitrogen saturating his blood doesn't have time to be carried to the lungs and breathed off. If outside pressures decrease too fast, the gas will come out of solution as bubbles right in the bloodstream. Carried to tiny vessels in the brain and spinal cord, they may cause circulation blockages and subsequent paralysis. Lodging in joints, they may cause pain and permanent bone damage.

Symptoms of decompression sickness include skin rash, general fatigue, speech defects and incoherence, headaches, dizziness, pain in the knees or elbows (this is called the bends), and severe breathing difficulty (the chokes). There is no hard-and-fast rule about who will be affected by decompression sickness and who won't. However, blood circulation is a strong factor in the elimination of excess nitrogen, and so older people with poor circulation tend to be more susceptible. Because of the solubility characteristics of nitrogen in fat, overweight people are also candidates. Scar tissue from past injuries can be build-up points for quantities of nitrogen. Divers who have been previously bent are more likely to be bent again. Intoxication, a hangover, fatigue, poor physical condition, hard work while at depth, and cold water all contribute to the possibility of bends.

No-Decompression Dives

Body tissues and blood assimilate nitrogen on every dive, of course, but at moderate depths and with short bottom times the body does not absorb enough of the gas for it to be a critical factor. Therefore, the best way to avoid decompression sickness is to avoid deep dives and not stay down too long. How long is *too* long? The U.S. Navy has determined that a diver who stays at 30 feet or less can remain down indefinitely without having to decompress when coming up. The deeper one goes below 30 feet, the less the time that can be spent there without decompression.

The following table gives allowable times at various depths for no-decompression dives. When studying the table, remember two important points: Ascents should always be made at 60 feet per minute—the speed of the smallest bubbles—to allow pressure to be reduced under control. And bottom time is not just the time spent at the bottom, but is counted from the moment a diver leaves the surface to the moment he leaves the bottom to begin ascent.

No-Decompression Limits

Depth in feet	Permissible bottom time
33 or less	No limit
35	310 minutes
40	200 minutes
50	100 minutes
60	60 minutes
70	50 minutes
80	40 minutes
90	30 minutes
100	25 minutes
110	20 minutes
120	15 minutes
130–140	10 minutes
150–190	5 minutes

The U.S. Navy is currently working on a new set of diving tables, which may cause these figures to be revised. Your diving instructor will advise you of any changes.

Repetitive Dives

A repetitive dive is one made within twelve hours of a previous dive. Each dive after the first during this time period puts a little more nitrogen into the body, and this must be taken into account to avoid the effects of residual nitrogen. Repetitive dive tables and a work sheet are given in the Appendix.

Decompression Dives

As mentioned before, just about anything of interest to the sport diver is in the relatively shallow depths. But sooner or later a diver may decide to stay down longer or go deeper than the no-decompression limits. Any dive that is beyond the limits of the no-decompression table requires decompression stops. The ascent must be delayed long enough to allow excess nitrogen to be removed from the body.

The diver contemplating a decompression dive must plan to have air available at certain depths, either in his own tank or through another source, such as a tank and regulator tied to a boat's anchor line or brought down by another diver. If stops are to be made, a watch and a depth gauge are essential, as well as a good buoyancy compensator vest to help hold position. The safe diver should plan decompression dives (see Chapter 6), not create the need for them by ignorance or carelessness.

MISCELLANEOUS DIVING ILLNESSES

Miscellaneous diving illnesses refer to problems not directly related to ascent or descent. They are a result of poor blood circulation, stress, excesses of certain components of air, or contamination of the air supply.

The Importance of Free Circulation

Unless blood can circulate freely to and within the brain, unconsciousness will occur. An inadequate blood supply can be caused by an overly tight wet-suit collar or hood that puts pressure on the carotid artery, situated at the side of the neck. Even a loose hood, when tucked in and zipped up tight, may restrict breathing and impede circulation on deeper dives.

A feeling of dizziness and rising body temperature are the body's warning to surface. The treatment for a diver who has fainted is fresh air and loosening of collar or jacket. Elevating the legs will help restore circulation in the brain. Most other diving maladies are a result of either too little or too much of the components of the air we breathe.

Fatigue and Diver Stress

Tiring swims, wounds, cold—even the physical strain of suiting up for a dive and wearing all the equipment—may cause fatigue or a stress situation followed by panic. Usually the first sign of panic is rapid, shallow breathing. This results in insufficient ventilation of the lungs and hypercapnia, an accumulation of carbon dioxide in the body.

The signs of hypercapnia are shallow breathing and dilation of the pupils. Often the victim has feelings of anxiety. Collapse usually follows. A diver experiencing early symptoms should terminate the dive and surface. After inflating his vest and dropping his weight belt, if necessary to keep his head above the water, he should breathe deeply to ventilate the lungs.

Anoxia—Not Enough Oxygen

Anoxia is a lack of sufficient amounts of oxygen in the body tissues. If the deficiency lasts long enough, cells will stop functioning and die; three to four minutes' delay in getting help will cause irreparable brain damage. Rarely associated with open-circuit scuba, anoxia is identified more with skin diving and with closed-circuit rebreathing equipment.

Hyperventilation—breathing deep and fast before submerging—purges carbon dioxide from the body and allows longer breath-holding time, which is a bonus for the skin diver. However, when hyperventilation is practiced to an excess, the body's oxygen level can drop dangerously low before the diver realizes it. Generally, there is no warning of oxygen starvation, and the diver may carry out normal functions right up to the point of unconsciousness.

The person hit with anoxia will experience a quickened pulse rate and the loss of fine muscle control. In addition, though it is difficult to notice when the victim is submerged, he will be cyanotic (blue) in color. Treatment is to have plenty of fresh air or oxygen. If breathing has stopped, artificial respiration should be given. Anoxia can be prevented by avoiding excessive hyperventilation and by not staying down beyond the point at which your body "demands" air. In other words, avoid breath-holding contests.

Oxygen Toxicity—Too Much Oxygen

The blood must have a constant supply of oxygen to sustain life. Yet too much of this essential gas can be harmful to a diver at depth, since it is the partial pressure of oxygen, not the percentage, that determines oxygen toxicity.

Oxygen tolerance varies from person to person, and even for an individual it is seldom consistent from day to day. The minimum amount of oxygen the average person can handle is not precisely known, but 2 atmospheres of oxygen seems to be the maximum the body can handle without side effects. When the partial pressure of oxygen is equivalent to 10 atmospheres, it is lethal.

In closed-circuit oxygen rebreathers—used chiefly by the military—the oxygen content is 100 percent, or 14.7 psi at 1 atmosphere, and 29.4 psi at 2 atmospheres. The U.S. Navy limits its divers using such apparatus to 25 feet for 75 minutes, which leaves a safety margin of about 25 percent, or 8 feet.

Sport divers should not fill their open-circuit tanks with pure oxygen because diving below 33 feet on oxygen alone is potentially dangerous, even for short periods.

The most common symptoms of oxygen poisoning are twitching, breathing difficulties, nausea, and tunnel vision. None of these effects is serious enough to cause death in itself, but drowning could result from the symptoms.

Carbon Dioxide Excess

A diver can create a condition of excessive carbon dioxide in his body through improper breathing. In an attempt to stretch the air in a tank, some divers will skip-breathe (hold their breath briefly between inhalation and exhalation) or breathe very shallowly, both of which inadequately ventilate the lungs and increase the partial pressure of carbon dioxide. Extreme physical exertion without proper respiration also increases the onset of carbon dioxide excess. If you notice labored breathing, accompanied by weakness, just relax and breathe in and out deeply a few times to flush excess carbon dioxide from your body.

Early symptoms of carbon dioxide excess include poor concentration and loss of coordination. After an attack many divers have been temporarily incapacitated by extreme headaches located just above the frontal sinus. Rest and breathing fresh surface air will relieve this condition.

Deaths from carbon dioxide excess are rare in open-circuit scuba; nevertheless, if carbon dioxide is allowed to build up to 10 percent, drowsiness and confusion may set in, followed by unconsciousness. Symptoms of increasing carbon dioxide levels at 1 atmosphere are listed below.

3%	Labored breathing, loss of concentration
6%	Panting
10%	Unconsciousness
15%	Convulsions

If your scuba gear is in good working order and you practice proper breathing techniques, you should never experience excessive carbon dioxide buildup.

Carbon Monoxide Poisoning

Carbon monoxide competes with oxygen for association with the blood hemoglobin (the respiratory component of red blood cells), and because it has a greater affinity for hemoglobin, it combines at a rate of about 300 to 1 over oxygen. When inhaled, carbon monoxide combines with the body's red blood cells to the point where oxygen can no longer be transported and tissues start to die from anoxia.

Carbon monoxide poisoning is caused when engine exhaust fumes are sucked into the compressor that is used to fill air cylinders, either from nearby autos or from the compressor engine itself. It can also come from faulty lubrication in the compressor.

Most state and local governments require strict adherence to air purity standards in filling diving cylinders. When traveling to remote areas for extensive diving, however, the safe diver will include a carbon monoxide analysis gauge as part of his gear. A concentration of 400 parts per million (.04 percent carbon monoxide in air) will cause symptoms during the first dive, and a concentration of 700 ppm (.07 percent), which is about 30 percent fluid saturation, will cause collapse. Symptoms are a "drunk" feeling, an increase in respiration, cyanotic skin, cherry-red lips and nails, and, finally, unconsciousness.

Immediate treatment is plenty of fresh air. If the victim is not breathing, mouth-to-mouth resuscitation should be started. Since carbon monoxide has such affinity for combining with the blood hemoglobin, most victims will need to be given oxygen to make up for the deficiency. The more severe cases may even require transfusion of fresh blood.

A Word of Reassurance

The foregoing discussion of diving diseases is not meant to instill fear but to make you alert to potential hazards. The wise and cautious diver isn't likely to be overcome by such maladies. Diving is a safe sport, as long as you make it so, and awareness of diving illnesses will enable you to avoid them.

Getting into a snug wet suit bottom is sometimes best done by having a friend shake you in.

5

Skin-diving Skills

Diving While Holding Your Breath

Skin diving, also known as breath-hold diving, is an ancient skill, carried on today much as it has been for centuries. For generation after generation the commercial ama divers of Japan have harvested abalone and pearl oysters on a lungful of air, and food-seeking Polynesians have made long, breath-holding dives to spear fish for food. As a sport, however, skin diving is only about forty-five years old, having started—as have so many underwater developments—on the French Riviera, as a competitive spearfishing game.

A dedicated skin diver is a purist, disdainful of donning anything other than a mask, snorkel, fins, and—only when absolutely necessary—an exposure suit. By holding his breath to dive rather than carrying a supply of air, the skin diver definitely limits himself in the marine environment, relying more on human ability and less on equipment. This kind of diver likes to be free and unencumbered and is not at all bothered by having to return to the surface to breathe.

101

USING THE FACE MASK

Unfortunately, few courses offer instruction in skin diving alone. One must either learn the skills through practical experience—such as going out with a friend—or take an entire diving course which merely begins with skin techniques as preliminary training for developing the more rigorous scuba methods. Because many of the fundamentals are basic to both skin and scuba diving, much of what is presented in this chapter applies also to scuba skills.

After selecting the mask that best fits you, prepare it for use by scrubbing the glass with toothpaste, baking soda, or mild detergent. Faceplates of new masks are often coated with a thin layer of oil or preservative, which must be removed for clear vision. Next, adjust the head strap for a snug, comfortable fit. If the glass presses against your nose, or if the flange makes red marks on your face, the strap is probably too tight. If you find the strap loosening when

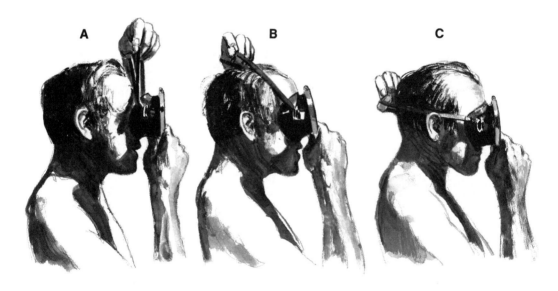

Donning a face mask. First hold the mask against your face, settling the flange comfortably around your eyes and under your nose (A). Holding the mask flat, pull the strap up and over your head (B). Pull the strap down in back, keeping it flat for maximum snugness (C).

it's wet, fasten the free ends by securing them flat at the buckles with a few turns of black plastic tape.

When donning your mask, dunk it in water first to assure a good seal to your face. Push your hair back from your forehead and with one hand hold the mask against your face. With the other hand, pull the strap over and down the back of your head. This method will prevent hair from getting caught between the mask and your face, which results in leakage.

It's a good practice to keep your mask on at all times when in the water, even if you're resting at the surface. If you do push it up for a minute while surface floating, keep a hand on it. Better yet, pull it down below your chin. Many a mask has been sent to the bottom as a result of rough water combined with a diver's carelessness.

One of the most important skin and scuba skills is mask clearing. If water should get into your mask, you're going to have to clear it out in order to see. On the surface this is easy—just pull the mask away from your face and empty the water. But below, moving the mask around at all is going to let more water in. Underwater clearing involves exhaling through the nose to displace water with air. It's a simple skill, but one that takes a little practice to master.

To practice clearing, sit on the bottom of the swimming pool in about 5 feet of water, with your buddy holding you down by placing both hands on your shoulders. Gently pull the top of the mask away from your face to let water flood it. Now tilt your head back until you're looking toward the surface at a 45-degree angle. Press the top of the mask against your forehead with one hand and gently and steadily exhale through your nose. Trapped water will be forced out along the bottom of the mask. To clear a mask with a purge valve, just tilt your head forward instead of back and force the water out by slowly exhaling through your nose. Pressing the mask against your face usually isn't necessary.

If the operation isn't a total success at first, don't be discouraged. Perhaps you allowed air to escape between your lips. Maybe you didn't tilt your head back far enough. Or you may have pushed too hard on the top of the mask and caused the bottom to lift from your face.

If you're in a horizontal swimming position underwater and need to clear, merely roll to either side so one shoulder is pointing up, press the side of the mask nearest the surface, and exhale through your nose. This method is used in wreck diving or working in a lobster or abalone hole.

By practicing mask clearing, you'll gain confidence in your own abilities, and the fear of flooding will be the least of your concerns. A skilled skin diver can clear a mask more than once on a single breath.

Mask clearing is an important skill that should be perfected through practice. First flood the mask by pulling it away from your face. Then tilt your head back and press the top of the mask against your forehead, as shown, while exhaling through your nose. It may take more than one breath to force all the water out of the bottom edge of the mask.

To clear a mask with a purge, first flood the mask by pulling it away from your face. Then hold it snugly against your face and simply exhale through your nose while tilting your head forward. The trapped water will be forced out of the purge.

USING THE SNORKEL

Many people enjoy swimming face down along the surface, breathing through a snorkel, while gazing at marine life. They are not divers and would be the first to acknowledge it, adding proudly that they are *snorkelers*. Their pleasure is in observing without diving. Skin and scuba divers are also snorkelers, but only until they find an appealing place to descend, or when they want to swim easily on the surface while conserving air. For either the skin or the scuba diver, a snorkel is an integral piece of equipment, a safety device as well as a convenience. It should always be attached to the mask, ready for use, not tucked into the weight belt or held in the hand.

With the snorkel fastened to the left side of your mask, its mouthpiece in your mouth, and your face looking down, the upper end of the tube should point back slightly and be just past your ear. The mouthpiece should feel comfortable, and you should be able to breathe easily at a normal rate. If the mouthpiece twists in your mouth or seems to be prying at your jaws, readjust the position of the tube in its keeper.

Practice floating face down, inhaling and exhaling through the snorkel without lifting your head. Swim around on the surface for a while to get used to breathing through your mouth. To descend, take a good breath, without filling your lungs to maximum capacity, and make a smooth surface dive, as is described later in this chapter, keeping the snorkel in your mouth. Water will enter the open end of the tube—you'll hear it gurgle in—but none should get into your mouth as long as your lips are sealed around the mouthpiece. If a little water does trickle in, block the mouthpiece opening with your tongue.

When you're ready to return to the surface, look up, extend your left arm above your head, and slowly rotate 360 degrees as you ascend to avoid overhead obstacles. A few feet from the surface, start with a slow, steady exhalation. With the snorkel tilted back, air will become trapped in the tube as the column of water is expelled. When your face breaks the surface, roll your head forward and continue breathing. If, while ascending, you desire to maintain eye contact with an object on the bottom, extend your left arm over your head and rise slowly, keeping your face down. As soon as the snorkel tip breaks the surface, give a sharp puff through your mouth to blow out the water.

If you're worried about gasping water into your snorkel when you come up, just remember that your lungs are full of air, and before you can breathe anything in, you have to breathe out. Exhaling forces water out of the snorkel and, as long as you're at the surface, the following inhalation brings you air, not water.

When you're bobbing about on the surface in choppy swells, some water may spill into the open end of your snorkel. Just keep your eyes on the waves and be prepared to blow out or swallow.

A technique worth practicing is snorkel breathing without a mask, a skill that builds self-assurance and that is not as difficult as it might sound. After settling the mouthpiece, gently lower your face into the water and breathe normally through your mouth. If you have difficulty, try exhaling slightly through your nose as it enters the water. This will create a negative pressure in the nasal cavity and encourage mouth breathing.

USING THE SWIM FINS

Swim fins give you two or three times more swimming efficiency than you enjoy with bare feet. However, their most important advantage is in conserving your strength and energy, not in increasing your speed.

Because walking is difficult when wearing fins, you should don them just before entering, as close to the water as surf conditions permit. On a beach, sit facing the water and slip them on, always holding both fins so one doesn't get washed away. (Remember, fins go on more easily if you wet them and your feet.) Or stand on one leg, leaning on your buddy for support. If you have to move on dry land while wearing fins, shuffle sideways or walk backward, glancing around to see where you're going.

When exiting, you can slip your fins off in the shallows and walk ashore if the water is very calm. Otherwise, crawl far up on the beach on hands and knees before removing them. On a boat do not attempt to walk about wearing fins; there is little enough room on deck without a diver's falling on it. Put your fins on just prior to entering the water and take them off before or right after getting out.

If you don't wear neoprene booties under your fins, a pair of heavy socks sometimes makes the fins more comfortable and prevents chafing during vigorous kicking.

Flutter Kick

The most widely used leg stroke in both skin and scuba diving is the flutter, a modified scissors kick covering an arc of 1 to 2 feet. The kick starts at your

To don fins on the beach, wet them and your feet, then move up the beach out of the water. With your buddy supporting you, pull one fin on, then the other. Help your buddy with the same procedure.

hip and travels down through a semiflexed knee and on to a loose ankle and pointed toes. Avoid overstressing the pointed toes or you may cramp your foot and leg muscles. The kick should be rhythmic and even, one leg going up as the other goes down. Don't stiffen your knees, but don't bend them too much either, or you'll start bicycling, which burns up energy and gets you nowhere.

The flutter kick is efficient both on the surface and underwater. It works quite satisfactorily for swimming on your back, giving a rest to the muscles used in swimming face down.

For all leg kicks, your arms should be relaxed and close to your body for minimum water resistance. If visibility is poor, you can extend one arm to avoid running into things.

The flutter kick is the most commonly used kick in diving. Keeping your legs reasonably straight without stiffening them, alternately move each up and down, starting the motion at the hips. Keep one arm at your side, the other outstretched as a protection against running into obstacles.

The dolphin kick requires both legs to be moved up and down together in a rhythmic movement that travels the length of the body. Most of the leg motion should come from the hips, the knees flexing easily but not bending sharply. Keep one arm at your side, the other outstretched.

Dolphin Kick

With the dolphin kick, both legs are held close together and move as one, starting with an up-and-down, undulating movement at the hips, which travels down the slightly flexed knees to the feet and fins. Because the dolphin kick gives maximum propulsion and calls for the greatest expenditure of energy, it should be used only as a change of pace. Being so energetic, it is effective in generating temporary warmth in cold water. The dolphin kick is easier and more efficient underwater than on the surface.

GETTING IN AND OUT OF A WET SUIT

Donning a wet suit may hardly seem a skill, but divers who wear the suits are quite familiar with the sometimes exasperating chore of tugging on a skintight outfit before each dive. Sometimes the struggle to get dressed for diving is so great that by the time the diver is ready to enter the water, he's too tired to do it.

To suit up, start out with the odds in your favor by choosing an area free of dirt, rocks, and loose sand; if you must dress on the beach, stand on a towel. A collection of miscellaneous debris under a snugly fitting wet suit is distinctly disturbing. For comfort, your bathing suit should be nylon, with flat seams, and have no exposed metal grommets, buttons, or zipper pulls to press into your flesh or catch on your wet suit. Putting your bathing suit on before leaving home will eliminate having to find dressing quarters at the dive site.

If your wet suit is the "skin" type, with no lining, you'll probably need to sprinkle the insides liberally with baby powder or cornstarch to facilitate pulling it on. Powder makes a mess, so be considerate of other divers when applying it. Wet-suit bottoms will go on much easier if you wear a pair of nylon pantyhose under them. Yes, this works well for men too.

Don the bottoms first, putting one leg through at a time and grasping large handfuls of material to pull it up. Be sure to get the pants hauled well up in the crotch and over the hips. (Long fingernails can be a hazard to a thin wet suit, and the chances of breaking them are good.) After your pants are on, make sure there aren't any creases behind the knees; work them out with the flat of your hands. Now put on your booties. They should be tucked *under* the pant legs to provide maximum warmth and to keep sand out.

Get into your jacket by putting one arm at a time into the sleeves. Again, smooth wrinkles out with your hands. If you are wearing instruments, put your compass on your right arm above the wrist, and your depth gauge on your left arm over your wet suit. Your diver's watch can go on your left wrist. If there are sleeve zippers, they generally fall to your buddy to zip up.

If the day is warm, or if you won't be diving for some time, don't zip your jacket right away because, once you're completely snugged up, your body temperature and pulse rate will rise quickly. If you get too warm, enter the water for a minute to cool off. If you feel worn out from suiting up, take a while to relax and calm down.

Hood and gloves go on last. For maximum protection, the skirt of the hood should go inside the jacket collar. Glove tops should go over the cuffs of your jacket; they're easier to put on and take off that way. Last of all, if your suit has a crotch flap (called a beaver tail), don't forget to fasten it.

When you're completely suited up, put on your buoyancy vest or stabilizer jacket with tank attached. Snug all straps enough that vest or jacket won't lift away from your body when they're inflated or when you move around underwater.

If you're using a power inflator, be sure to connect it and turn the air on at the tank valve. Don't wait until you're in the water.

Last of all, put on your weight belt by laying it flat on the ground and picking it up behind you, holding an end in each hand. Bend over from the hips and gently lay the belt across your back, then fasten the buckle in front. Don't throw it up on your back—that hurts. You may have to readjust the bottom of your BC vest so that the weight belt fits over its strap but doesn't catch the vest itself. Be sure that the weight belt and its buckle are not covered by anything. If you have to ditch your belt, it must drop free immediately.

Getting out of your gear is easier than getting into it. Release the buckle of your weight belt and, holding onto it, ease it down to the beach or boat deck. If you just drop it, it may land on a foot. Peel your wet suit off, turning it wrong side out. Get your buddy to help pull if sleeves or legs are stubborn.

HOW TO ENTER THE WATER

Getting into the water when wearing diving gear requires somewhat more style than making a whooping run down the beach or a headlong plunge off a boat. Swim fins are too awkward on dry land to permit the former method, and the possibility of dislodging one's face mask eliminates the latter. Certain basic

To don a weight belt, lay it flat on the ground behind you. Then pick up an end in each hand and swing it gently across your back, fastening the buckle in front. The weight belt is always the *last* piece of gear to go on.

entries have, through use, proved efficient for either the skin- or scuba-equipped diver.

Giant Stride

The giant stride is used for entry off a boat deck when a ladder or a diving platform is not available, or off a dock as high as 5 feet above the surface. Because you don't submerge immediately with this entry, it is recommended when the depth of the water is unknown or visibility is restricted.

A little air in your BC vest will give you positive buoyancy. Stand erect with snorkel (or regulator) in your mouth, supporting your face mask with one hand and keeping your elbow close to your chest. Extend your other arm to the side for balance and braking when striking the water. Take a breath and, holding your body straight, step well forward, keeping the leading fin pointed slightly upward. Keep the other leg back until both feet touch the water, then bring your legs together vigorously in scissors fashion, which will prevent you from sinking deeply. Fixing your eyes on some object in front of you will help maintain proper body position. Done properly, without jumping, this entry will keep you at the surface; you won't even get your head wet.

A variation on the giant stride is the feet-together entry, used when the distance to the water is greater than about 5 feet. Start in the same manner as before, but when you are in midair, close the scissors of your legs so you hit the water with both feet together, fins pointing slightly upward. Your outstretched arm will brake you somewhat, but you will sink a couple of feet, so be prepared to hold your breath longer and clear your snorkel, or start breathing on scuba.

As comical as it seems, some divers have forgotten to don their fins before entering the water.

Giant stride entry. Stand with feet together, then step out and topple forward without jumping. Both feet will enter the water almost at the same time; when they do, bring them together scissors fashion to keep your head above the surface. Have the snorkel or regulator in your mouth and hold it and your face mask with one hand to keep them from being dislodged.

Forward Roll

This entry is quite effective from a boat when pitching or rolling movements prevent you from standing balanced for a giant stride. Facing the water, sit or squat at either the boat's railing or stern, with your chin tucked down between your knees and your heels pulled in close to your body. Your snorkel or regulator should be in your mouth. Hold your face mask with both hands, keep your elbows in, and roll forward into the water, landing on your back. Be sure to keep your legs bent and knees close to your chest until you're in the water.

This entry will take you underwater a couple of feet. You may feel a slight bit of disorientation, owing to spinning of inner-ear fluids when you turn over, but the sensation will pass in a couple of seconds.

Forward roll entry. Bend at the waist and at the knees and simply fall forward in this position, keeping arms, legs, and head tucked close to your body until you're in the water. Any push-off or jumping action will guarantee a belly flop. Hold your face mask to your face during entry.

Back roll entry. A forward roll in reverse. Bending at the waist and at the knees, roll back, keeping your knees pulled up close to your chest. Don't worry about getting water in your nose; your face mask will prevent that from happening as long as you hold it to your face.

Back Roll

The back roll is just the reverse of the front roll. It is an excellent entry from a small boat where standing up is impractical or hazardous, or from a boat with a high railing. It is effective when you're holding cameras or other equipment. Sitting at the railing with your back to the water, just fall back while pulling your knees up toward your chest and your heels toward your buttocks, maintaining this tucked position until you're in the water. Support your face mask with one hand, leaving the other free to hold gear. Again, any dizziness will disappear once you're upright in the water.

Exercise caution when making this entry, to be sure no one is in the water behind you.

Beach Entry

A beach entry can be merely a matter of wading into calm water and pulling on your fins when you're waist deep (around algae-covered rocks, watch where you step, and beware of sea urchins), or it may involve a carefully thought out surf approach. If waves are roaring in and pounding onto the beach, or if you are at all unsure of yourself, don't attempt to enter but look for a calmer locale. Before any beach entry, scout the area first to find a place where the surf is rolling in low rather than dumping down hard. Watch the natural wave rhythm. Usually there will be a lull, a series of moderate-sized waves followed by a couple of big ones. The best time to enter is after the big waves have finished or after the ebb of a medium one.

Put your fins on at the water's edge, then slowly back down into the water, watching for rocks or holes. Look over your shoulder at the incoming waves and keep your knees bent to absorb their force. Waiting until after a modest-sized wave breaks and the water is about knee high and flowing out, turn quickly, supporting your face mask with one hand, and dive deep. Swim out strongly for 10 or 15 feet close to the bottom, then surface and rejoin your buddy.

For a surf entry, hold your buddy's hand (A) and shuffle backward into the water, looking behind you for underwater obstacles or waves (B&C). When the water is about knee-high, wait for the outflow of a medium-sized wave (D), then turn and dive deep (E). Swim underwater, parallel to your buddy, for about 10 feet, then surface to make sure you're still both together.

Looking toward the surface from 100 feet down a drop-off wall in the Bahamas, buddies stay in visual contact.

If you have a float, let it trail behind you on a 6- to 8-foot nylon line so it will ride over the tops of the waves. Attempting to ride through surf on a mat or an inner tube may lead to a dumping and possible loss of gear.

Various shore configurations and recommended ways of entry and exit are discussed in Chapter 7.

RESTING ON THE SURFACE

Getting to a diving spot may require a long, snorkeling swim from shore or a boat, and you may need a rest on the way. Or, while diving, you may want to relax on the surface for a while to warm up or talk with your buddy. There are several methods of surface resting, all of them quite simple. Some depend on equipment, such as a float or your buoyancy compensator vest; others rely on your own ability as a floater (see the discussion on drownproofing in Chapter 2).

To rest with an inner tube or a surf mat, just hang on, leaving your body in the water, or else haul yourself up on it face down, using your feet for propulsion. If you aren't using a surface float, inflate your BC vest in the following manner: Take a deep breath and, with your right hand, remove your snorkel from your mouth. With your left hand, grasp your vest's oral inflator and blow into it. One or two good breaths should do the trick, but if you get winded, stop puffing and snorkel breathe until you get your breath back.

Whenever resting on the surface, keep your eyes on where you are—how far from the shore or your boat, how far up or down the beach—to make sure you don't drift out of a safe swim-back distance.

GETTING BELOW THE SURFACE

The most widely used and most efficient dive for descending in unobstructed water is the jackknife. Executed correctly, it carries you straight down with a minimum of effort.

Take in a breath of air and, with your arms at your sides, merely bend down from the waist and extend both legs over your head, keeping them fairly straight. The weight of your legs will be enough to drive you well below the surface, where you can use your fins for going deeper. The jackknife dive should be done in one smooth, continuous movement: inhale, invert, and swing your legs up.

The jackknife dive is done smoothly while swimming at the surface either when snorkeling or on scuba. Keeping your legs straight at the knees, bend from the waist to bring your head down. Then stretch your legs almost straight up and bring your arms forward. The more you extend your legs out of the water, the deeper you'll be driven down.

PIKE DIVE

JACKKNIFE DIVE

The pike dive is a variation on the jackknife. Instead of keeping your legs straight, pull your knees in toward your chest and roll over head down. As soon as you're upside down, thrust your legs up.

If you can't see down into the water to tell if there are rocks or other obstructions, or if you are surrounded by marine growth and don't have enough room for a jackknife or pike dive, the feet-first dive works well. This is known as the kelp dive in California waters, the vertical drop in some other diving

A pike dive begins at the surface, as for the jackknife. However, for the pike, draw your knees up to your chest while turning head down. Then quickly straighten your legs and thrust them high to drive yourself down, stretching your arms forward to guard against running into obstacles.

A   B

The kelp dive. Use when marine growth restricts your movement. First clear a space in the canopy by pushing the kelp aside. With arms outstretched, spread your legs (A), then bring them together in a strong scissors motion while pushing down with the palms of both hands (B). This will lift your upper body out of the water (C). As you begin to drop back, drive yourself down by pushing up strongly with the palms of your hands until your arms are outstretched over your head (D & E).

circles. Starting from an upright position, with arms outstretched, give a strong scissors kick with your legs while pushing down against the water with the palms of both hands. This action will lift you out of the water. As you start back down, take a breath and, keeping your body straight, push up toward the surface with both arms as soon as your shoulders are submerged. If you are positively buoyant, you may need to make several arm motions to get under, but if you're weighted properly, you'll sink deeply enough to roll forward underwater and begin swimming. When descending in a kelp bed, first push the kelp away from you to clear a "hole" for entry.

Finally, if you have trouble equalizing the pressure in your ears (see following pages), you may prefer a feet-first descent.

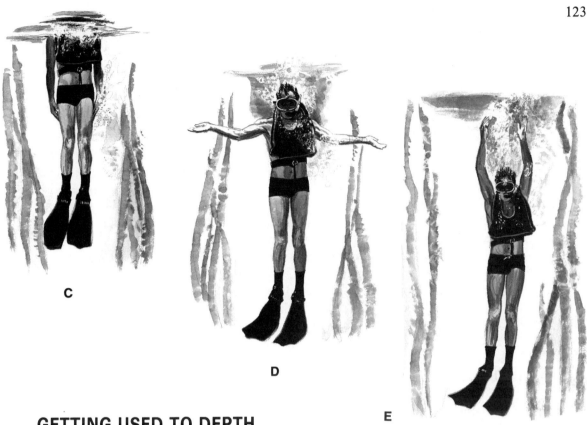

C

D

E

GETTING USED TO DEPTH

As soon as you begin to descend below the surface, you should be prepared for pressure changes—called "squeeze"—that will affect certain areas of your body. Squeeze has been covered in detail in Chapter 4. Since the body is made up of approximately 70 percent incompressible fluids, most of it can withstand great changes in pressure. However, the body also contains some spaces in which compressible air is trapped, and discomfort may result unless these spaces are equalized, or balanced, with increasing surrounding pressure. Such air pockets exist in the middle ear, the nasal cavities or sinuses, and the lungs. Following are some practical tips on pressure equalization.

Middle Ear and Sinus Squeeze

The middle ear is a space between the eardrum and the Eustachian tube (a passage connected to the throat). Before submerging, the middle ear contains air at surface pressure. With increasing depth and its increasing external pressure, the differential across the eardrum is felt first as a dull pushing-in sensation on the ears, then as an increasingly sharp pain. This discomfort is an early warning signal. If you do not heed it and immediately balance the internal pressure of your middle ear with the surrounding water pressure, pain may give way to a ruptured eardrum.

To equalize such pressure, pinch your nostrils shut and try to exhale gently through your nose. Air will be forced from the breathing passages through the Eustachian tubes into the middle ear, offsetting the pressure that is forcing your eardrum inward. You may experience a light popping or squeaking in the ears; this indicates proper equalization. If you have difficulty equalizing, turn your head from side to side and swallow. Also try yawning with your mouth shut, or moving your jaw back and forth. Flooding your mask and clearing it by exhaling through your nose is often effective.

If you can't equalize the first time or two, don't lose hope. Several dives on succeeding days may be necessary to actually stretch the eardrum, making it more flexible and thus more easily equalized.

Equalization should start within the first 6 feet of descent to prevent the Eustachian tube from possibly collapsing and closing the air passage. A good rule is: Start equalizing *before* you feel the need to.

The sinuses are air-filled spaces in the front part of the skull. As with the ears, internal pressure of the sinuses must remain in equilibrium with external water pressure. Sinus squeeze is felt as a sharp pinch above the eyes or behind the nose and is usually taken care of when the ears are equalized. Even with proper equalization, however, sinus squeeze may cause a small amount of blood to be forced from your nose into your face mask, giving you an anxious moment when you first become aware of it. Never dive when you have a cold or any nasal congestion. At such times swollen tissues may block the sinuses altogether, and forceful exhalation may drive fluids into the inner ear, causing damage.

Decongestant nose drops, sprays, or tablets can be effective in reducing congestion. However, different people react differently to medication, so before using any "sure cures," talk with a diving instructor or your doctor. If blockages persist over a period, be sure to see your doctor.

Lung Squeeze

As a skin diver descends, holding his breath, the amount of air in his lungs is compressed by one-half in the first 33 feet. Continued descent results in continued compression. In the past it was assumed that descent below this point was harmful, but current studies have disproved that belief. Unless you drop into deep water holding an anchor or a large rock, you're not likely to go down far enough for lung squeeze to be of any concern.

Underwater Breath-Holding

Depending on water temperature and on one's bodily exertion underwater, a skin diver in good condition can stay under for close to a minute on a single breath of air. The colder the water is, the shorter the time one can stay down, because the body uses up great quantities of energy just in keeping warm. And the more a diver moves around, pursuing fish or prying abalone, the faster energy is burned up. Under ideal conditions—for example, holding perfectly still on the bottom in tropical waters—an experienced skin diver could remain below for two minutes or longer.

Your body burns fuel (oxygen) in direct proportion to its activity. But if your muscles are tense, you also use oxygen just in keeping them rigid and thus decrease your breath-holding time. Underwater, try to swim smoothly and efficiently, avoiding unnecessary movements. Use your legs in a slow, relaxed manner. Keep your arms close to your sides until you need to use your hands. Relax your bite on your snorkel mouthpiece.

Of course, the more you practice breath holding, the more you can train your body and thus extend your underwater time. Deep breathing done several times a day is not only good for general health, since it cleanses little-used areas of the lungs, it also activates more of the lungs' tiny air cells, actually increasing breathing capacity. Underwater games (see the section Skin-Diving Games and Water Fun later in this chapter) are beneficial in that they get you breathing deeply and also take your mind off your respiration. Overall physical conditioning through lap swimming, distance running, and bike tripping helps build stamina and increase lung capacity.

Hyperventilation, or forced breathing, is a technique practiced by most divers to extend underwater time. Done correctly, it can be very effective. Done improperly, it can be a cause of death.

Hyperventilation involves inhaling and exhaling deeply three or four times before submerging. The rapid breathing washes carbon dioxide out of the lungs, reducing it to a low level, and causes more oxygen than normal to be forced into the blood. Because the technique does extend underwater time significantly, it is an important skill. However, you should be aware of the physiological concepts involved and the potential hazards of hyperventilation, some of which have already been discussed in Chapter 4.

Rapid deep breathing gives the body a pleasant tingling feeling; however, if done to an excess, hyperventilation may cause a temporary lightheadedness and even blackout at or near the surface. As if that weren't enough, during breath holding underwater, the breathing stimulus is lost and a diver actually loses the desire to breathe until it's too late. By then the body has used up all but about 10 percent of its oxygen, and the diver loses consciousness and drowns.

Hyperventilation should be practiced, but wisely. Inhale and exhale in slow, measured breaths rather than panting air in and out of your lungs. Limit the number of breaths to three or four. On the last breath, don't inflate your lungs to maximum capacity (it will make you too buoyant, anyway). Don't hyperventilate every time before a dive. After a dive, rest for a minute or so on the surface, breathing normally to allow your system to reach equilibrium.

THE DANGER OF DIVING ALONE

The practice of always diving with a buddy is such a basic rule that it should be engraved indelibly on your mind. If you dive alone, you're inviting trouble. When you're in the water by yourself, there is no one to lend a hand if you get tossed around in surf, no one to assist if you become exhausted a hundred yards out from shore, no one to help if you get tangled in marine growth, or snagged on a rock, or thrown against a reef.

The rule is simple, but it bears repeating many times over: *Never dive alone.*

EXITING FROM THE WATER

When piloting an airplane, taking off and flying around are only part of the picture because no flight can be called a total success until the pilot has made a safe landing. Diving is like flying in this regard. An easy entry and a good dive don't mean much if you can't get yourself back out of the water.

Especially in ocean diving, conditions tend to change during the time you're in the water, making your exit a fresh challenge. Currents may shift; waves may increase; you may be fatigued. For these and other reasons, you

To exit around rocks, swim forward slowly, looking alternately above and below water for obstacles. Keep your arms outstretched to fend yourself off obstacles. When the water surges, swim toward shore; when it recedes, hang onto a rock to prevent being carried back by the outflow. In this fashion keep working your way into the shallows, where you can crawl up onto the beach or onto a rock to remove your fins.

should always be prepared to modify your planned exit site, taking into account altered natural conditions and being prepared for any eventuality.

When exiting from the water onto a boat, don't try to crawl aboard wearing all your gear. If you've been collecting or spearfishing, let someone on deck take your game bag and catch to free your hands. Remove your fins and pass them up too. From there on, it's fairly easy to climb up a ladder or scramble over the boat's transom. When rough seas are pitching the boat up and down, stay clear when it rolls in your direction, then, at its lowest point, grab hold of the railing and heave yourself up before it lifts again.

Exiting onto a beach through surf requires a cool head and some fore-thought. Just outside the breaker zone, stop for a minute or two to rest and have a look around. Check that your equipment is secure and your BC vest is inflated just enough to give you positive buoyancy. Watch the wave action. Once you're sure of a period of relatively low waves between big ones, head toward shore, swimming strongly but not so hard you'll exhaust yourself. In the event you feel yourself in real danger, ditch your weight belt immediately.

As you move in, watch for breaking waves behind you. If a big one rears up over your head, hold your mask with one hand to keep it from being torn off, dive deep and let the wave dump, then surface and continue swimming. Once you get going, keep moving toward shore—don't hesitate in the surf line. When you hit the beach, dig in and hang on against the backwash, then crawl forward with each onrush.

Scuba-diving Skills

Diving with Air on Your Back

Not until you have mastered the skills of free diving—diving with mask, snorkel, and fins—should you get near the water with scuba. Too many eager swimmers have done a little snorkeling in a sheltered cove, a little splashing around in a lake, and, entranced by what they saw beneath the surface, put on a tank just to "take it down for a little look." In doing so, they have taken their lives in their hands by not knowing the proper use of self-contained breathing apparatus.

Scuba is not a toy. It should not be played with, nor should it be handled by anyone not properly trained in its use. Ignorance, carelessness, and any attitude short of a healthy respect for scuba can put your life on the line.

GETTING YOURSELF TOGETHER

Assuming that, as a safe diver, you have undergone safe training from a qualified instructor, take a few minutes before each dive to plan what you are going to do before you get into the water as well as after you're in it. By thinking ahead, you'll enjoy your dive more and any surprises will be the pleasant kind. This sort of preplanning should be carried out with your buddy before either of you dons equipment.

129

Buddies should assist each other before entering the water, making sure that all straps are snug, buckles fastened, zippers closed, instruments secure, and tank air turned on.

Study the water conditions from shore. Plan your entry and exit. Discuss where you are going and what you are going to do, how deep you expect to dive, how long you anticipate staying in the water. All this takes only a short while, but it is time well spent. Don't wait until you're in the water to talk things over—save your breath and energy for diving.

CHECKING OUT YOUR EQUIPMENT

Check your equipment. Do you have a full tank of air? Do you have a reserve valve on your tank, in good working order, or else a submersible pressure gauge that reads correctly? Do you have the proper amount of weight on your belt for neutral buoyancy in the water? Do you have all the instruments you'll need, such as underwater compass, depth gauge, watch? Is everything—including your own body—functioning properly?

Now get into your diving gear. First, put on your protective suit, if you need to wear one, except for hood and gloves. Don your buoyancy compensator next. Inspect your tank's backpack to make certain that the cylinder is secure. With most arrangements, the point where the valve threads into the tank should be even with the top of the backpack. If the tank rides higher, the valve may bump the back of your head. Any lower and you may not be able to reach up and back to retrieve the regulator hose. Check the scuba harness, its straps and buckles, to make sure that nothing is twisted and that the quick-release buckle works. Pull out the shoulder straps far enough that you can slip into the harness easily.

Inspect your regulator hose for signs of deterioration, especially at the points where it enters the first- and second-stage fittings. Remove the dust cap from the high-pressure seat and inspect the seat for moisture or foreign matter. Check the tank valve seat to make sure that the "O" ring is in good condition and in place.

Now stand your tank up in front of you with the straps of the backpack and the tank valve seat facing away from you. Fit the regulator high-pressure seat gently into the tank valve seat, with the regulator hose hanging down on the right and the submersible pressure gauge—if you're using one—on the left. Screw the mounting nut only finger tight; clamping down hard on it isn't necessary and may damage the "O" ring. Open the air valve gradually all the way, then back down half a turn. Check the pressure gauge to see if it's reading. If there is any air escaping around the "O" ring, you'll hear it. Sometimes a

A   B

Overhead tank donning is done in one smooth, continuous movement.
With the regulator in your mouth to keep it off the ground, place the tank
at your feet with the straps facing away from you. Reach down *through* the
straps and grasp the tank below its midpoint (A). Now lift the tank over your
head while straightening up (B), and let it slide gently down your back (C)
until the straps settle on your shoulders (D).

slight repositioning of the first stage will stop a leak; otherwise, you'll have to
replace the "O" ring.

At this point, you may suffer an overwhelming desire to purge the
regulator, just to hear the businesslike blast of air. Control the urge to purge

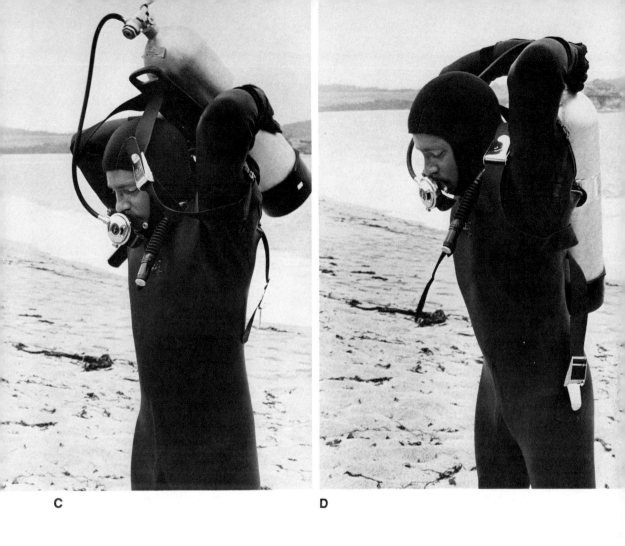

C   D

(it wastes air) and, instead, exhale into the mouthpiece. If your breath flows smoothly, then inhale. Always exhale first, to clear out any drops of water that may have gotten into the mouthpiece. Sometimes, when a regulator has been stored unused for a length of time, the one-way exhaust valve will stick shut and a vigorous exhalation will be needed to break the seal. This can usually be avoided by proper rinsing after each dive, draining, and drying out before storing.

Now, with your buddy's help, slip easily into your tank harness just as you would put on a coat, snug up the straps, and fasten the buckle under your buoyancy compensator vest. An alternate way of donning and doffing a tank is the overhead method. With the tank standing up and the straps facing away

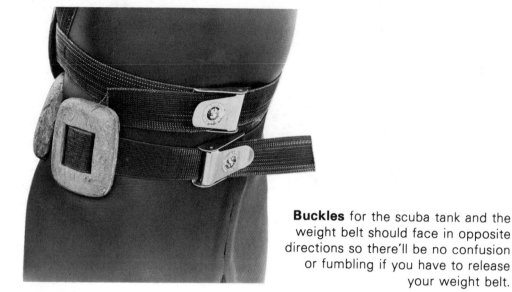

Buckles for the scuba tank and the weight belt should face in opposite directions so there'll be no confusion or fumbling if you have to release your weight belt.

from you, bend over from the waist and, reaching your arms well into the harness, grasp the tank between your hands. Stand up straight, lift the tank over your head, and let it down behind your head as the straps settle into place on your shoulders. Shrug the harness into position, having your buddy lift up on the tank if necessary, tighten the waist belt, and fasten the buckle. This overhead method takes a little practice but is preferred by many divers. Just be careful that no one is standing close behind you when you swing the tank over your head.

Don your hood, gloves, fins, mask, and—last of all—your weight belt. The weight belt always goes on last so it will drop free if it has to be ditched. Check your body to make sure that all straps are snug and free of entanglement, that zippers are closed, and that hoses are hanging loose. As a final check before entering the water, ask your buddy to make sure your air valve is on, and, if you're using a constant reserve valve, to make sure the handle is *up*.

SWIMMING ON THE SURFACE

Entries are discussed in Chapter 5, Skin-diving Skills, and they are made the same way when wearing scuba gear. When entering from the beach, you should be breathing from your regulator as you back into the water. Dropping in from a boat, support your regulator in your mouth with one hand, your mask to your face with the other hand. When entering from the boat, don't descend to depth the minute you hit the water but pause on the surface to take stock of yourself once more. Inflate your vest to make you buoyant and to help keep your snorkel above water. Look around and fix a visual bearing on a landmark or the boat. Move relaxedly and easily, without fighting the water, so as not to tire yourself.

When swimming along the surface, breathe through your snorkle to conserve your air supply. Your regulator should hang back over your right shoulder or else be attached to your buoyancy vest with a quick release device. Regulator neck straps are not advisable because they are difficult to release when the hands are cold, and they may become tangled in weeds or kelp.

Use a slow and steady flutter kick for surface swimming for the greatest conservation of energy and the most efficient propulsion. Keep an eye on waves that may fill your snorkel, or surges that may carry you into rocks.

Approaching shore, when you want to read the waves, switch to a sidestroke or swim on your back, in which case the snorkel will have to be removed from your mouth. Short glances over your shoulder will help maintain direction.

DESCENDING TO DEPTH

When you are ready to descend, move the regulator to your mouth. If it's drifting around behind you and you can't find it, reach up and back with your right hand, pushing your elbow with your other hand if your arm isn't loose-jointed enough. Grasp the hose at the tank valve and extend your arm, slipping your hand along the hose to the second stage. Exhale through the mouthpiece and start a slow breathing rhythm. After several breaths, release the air in your vest and start your descent. Remember that it's possible to sink straight down; you may not need to make a surface dive.

You should sink at the rate of about 75 feet per minute but never faster than you can equalize pressure. Proper equalization during the first 10 to 30 feet is very important. If you cannot clear at these depths, ascend a few feet to relieve the pressure and try again. As you approach two atmospheres absolute (33 feet), the pressure will reduce the air cells in a wet suit, making you negatively buoyant. If you begin to sink too fast, spread your legs to slow your

Boat diving is popular, whether from an inflatable craft or a large vessel. Divers can move around the surface with little effort, as well as change diving areas quickly. A diver should be familiar with the special skills required by boat exits and entries.

descent and put a few puffs of air into your vest. Make sure that your weight belt buckle remains in front of your body, as belts have a tendency to shift around when you undergo a squeeze. Even without a wet suit, you will become slightly negative below 33 feet, especially if you are wearing just enough weight to compensate for the buoyancy of your air cylinder as it empties. If your mask floods, merely purge the water clear by exhaling through your nose.

Keep an eye on your buddy during descent. If he has trouble equalizing, wait for him.

SWIMMING UNDERWATER AND SURFACING

Having reached the depth at which you plan to swim, check with your buddy that everything is okay and establish the direction you want to go. Move along side by side, maintaining constant visual contact. Swim a few feet off the bottom so as not to stir up sand or silt, and avoid excessive exertion by using smooth, even leg strokes, using your hands only to carry extra gear or to maintain directional control. As interested as you may become in the bottom, be sure to look ahead from time to time to avoid swimming headlong into rocks or other obstructions.

In the open underwater world the first—or hundredth—time, able to breathe, completely weightless, you may become enthralled with your surroundings. Sit down on the bottom, relax, gaze around, and enjoy yourself. If you feel like giving vent to your exuberance, do a gentle somersault in midwater, or stand on your head, or swim a way on your back, looking up at the surface.

Throughout your dive keep a constant check on your air supply. If your tank has a constant reserve, surface as soon as you go on reserve. Otherwise, surface when your pressure gauge reads 300 to 500 pounds. Always terminate a dive with a reserve of air in your tank in case you need it in exiting from the water.

When either you or your buddy is ready to terminate a dive, give the "thumbs-up" signal. Be sure to get an OK signal before kicking off. In rising to the surface at a controlled rate, never exceed 60 feet per minute, which is about the speed of your smallest air bubbles.

As you go up, breathe easily, holding your regulator to your mouth with your right hand. Extend your left hand above your head, look straight up, and make a few 360-degree rotations while rising to check topside for obstructions, such as a boat or a dock. There are few things as humiliating or painful as coming up under your own boat.

If there is air in your vest, bleed it off gradually by opening the mouthpiece valve. If you don't allow expanding air to escape (remember, you put the air in at depth, at a greater pressure), it may burst the vest. Breathe normally and do not hold your breath.

If you've controlled your ascent properly, you'll break the surface gently. Popping way out of the water in a great rush of bubbles may look dramatic to an observer who doesn't know any better, but it's a sure sign of an unskillful diver.

MAKING A SAFE EXIT

Once in the water, you have to get out. Exiting onto a boat is easier if you first remove your tank and hand it aboard along with your fins. If you prefer to keep your tank on, ask someone to give you an assist up, then try to lean forward over the boat's railing so you don't lose your balance and topple back.

In calm water you may want to snorkel all the way in to the beach. Exiting in surf in full scuba gear is half the fun of a dive, or half the battle, depending on how you look at it. The procedure for a safe exit is straightforward and not at all complicated. Again, the key is to remain calm.

First of all plan your exit. Know where you want to come out of the water and stick to a direct route to that spot unless circumstances force a change of plan. Stop outside the surf line and at the surface take stock of yourself and your gear. Set a compass heading if you're not confident of being able to swim a straight line underwater. When ready, let the air out of your vest and sink all the way to the bottom.

Swim easily toward shore, staying close to the bottom and keeping your course perpendicular to the wave motion unless you have to angle across a longshore current. At a sandy beach, as you enter the surf line, you'll note ripples on the bottom; as long as you move along *across* them, you'll be moving toward the beach.

Keep swimming, watching the bottom as well as looking ahead. At the point where the water begins foaming and you lose sight of the bottom because of stirred-up sand, be prepared for turbulence and the possibility of violent action. When you feel a definite backwash pulling at you, you're in the shallows. Grab the bottom to hold on against the outflow, crawling forward on hands and knees with each forward surge. In a few seconds you'll feel your back and head break the surface and you'll rejoice. But be prepared. Often one grand, final breaker will slam down squarely on top of you just as you're sure you're home free and roll you head over heels. If that happens, don't fight back, but

When making a beach exit, keep the regulator mouthpiece in your mouth and crawl on your hands and knees until you're well above the waterline, staying close to your buddy all the way. A regulator dragging in the surf or across the beach is sure to pick up large amounts of sand.

hang onto your face mask and get your hands and knees under you, then head onto shore and start crawling again.

Even when you feel clear of the waves and backwash and can see daylight all around, don't stand up, and be sure to keep your regulator mouthpiece in your mouth. You have much more control when your center of gravity is low, and dragging a regulator through sand won't do it a bit of good. Continue crawling until you are completely out of the water, then flop over, sit up, and congratulate yourself on a safe exit.

When making an exit on a rocky shore with surf, stay as close to the bottom as you can for as long as you can—at least until you're well inshore from the surf line. As you swim along, keep both arms outstretched to push yourself away from rocks or absorb the shock of contacting one. Once you're in relatively calm water at a depth of a couple of feet, stand up and back out. Be sure to glance over your shoulder to watch where you're going. If you remove your fins, slip the straps over one arm for safekeeping.

FINDING YOUR WAY BY COMPASS

You're not likely to get lost underwater, and if during a dive you should become disoriented and suffer the uneasy feeling of not being quite sure of where you are, go to the surface, put some air into your vest, relax for a few minutes, and take a look around. If you aren't wearing a compass and have a long haul back to shore, choose a clearly visible landmark, such as a high hill or a large, distinguishable rock, and swim easily toward it, breathing on snorkel. Glance up once in a while to make sure you're still aimed in the right direction. If you don't keep your mind on what you're doing and just swim aimlessly, you're likely to thrash around in circles, getting nowhere at all and tiring yourself out in the process.

Better than swimming toward a destination on the surface, however, is swimming to it the easy way by following a compass heading underwater. You will conserve air and minimize the need to surface to find out where you are, thus giving you maximum underwater time. Besides, it's more fun.

To set a simple compass heading, first float horizontally at the surface, looking directly at your dive boat or at a landmark in line with your beach destination. Wearing your compass on your right wrist, stretch your left arm straight out in front of you, pointing it toward your destination. Hold that arm parallel with the long axis of your body and grasp it just above the elbow with your right hand. Keep your right forearm perpendicular to your left upper arm, forming a kind of rectangle in front of your face. This should bring the compass directly in front of your eyes.

Now sight over the compass, aiming its lubber line (the fixed line) at your destination and swinging your entire body to get a good lineup. Note where the north arrow points and, keeping that right forearm squarely in front of you, use your left hand to align the indicator on the movable bezel with the north arrow. Now stretch out your left arm again, grasp it with your right hand, and once more point the lubber line at the target. Adjust the movable bezel, if necessary, to put its indicator exactly on the north arrow. Once all is adjusted, don't change your compass unless you take a reading for a new heading.

To follow a compass heading, either at the surface or underwater, stretch out your left arm, grasp it with your right hand, swing your body around until the compass bezel and the north arrow line up, and swim along in the direction the lubber line points. Remember to keep your body horizontal and straight in the water and to keep the lubber line exactly parallel to the longitudinal axis of your body and thus in the direction of movement. Also, to stay correctly oriented in regard to position and direction, sight *over* and *along* the compass rather than down on it.

Crosscurrents will tend to swing you off course, so you must compensate by heading slightly into them, the amount depending on their strength and direction. It's best to wear only your compass on your right arm, because metallic instruments or objects next to it may cause deviations.

A detailed treatment of basic navigational techniques is given in *Underwater Navigation for the Scuba Diver* by Jack E. Glatt, published and copyrighted in 1960 by the author.

Proper training, good planning, and constant preparedness are essential to safe scuba. It's not only *what* happens that can get a diver into trouble; it's how the diver reacts to the situation. If the first reaction is to "get the hell out of there" as fast as possible, that instinctive act of self-preservation may be the absolutely wrong move. Throughout a dive, always be on the alert, ready to respond coolly to any situation.

If you should be confronted by an emergency such as equipment failure (which is unlikely) or running out of air (which is more probable, if you haven't kept a close watch on it), the most vital thing you can do is to remain calm and think out the situation. Blindly rushing toward the surface could cause grave harm to you and others. A few seconds is generally all you need to evaluate the problem and take corrective measures. Whatever you do, don't ditch your tank unless it becomes hopelessly entangled: expanding air in the cylinder can give you that extra breath you may need while surfacing.

How to Clear Your Regulator

On occasion your regulator mouthpiece may become flooded. With a single-hose regulator simply exhale into the mouthpiece to purge the water. If you are too exhausted to exhale, just press the button. With a double-hose regulator, in addition to exhaling, roll to your left so the water will run into the exhaust hose. Your first inhalation should then be made with some caution, since there may be a little water left in the hose. You can swallow leftover water or you can lift the mouthpiece above your head where a free flow of air will purge it. After free flowing, turn down the mouthpiece to prevent water from rushing back in, then tilt your head back and move the mouthpiece down to your mouth.

In very turbid water the regulator exhaust valve may stay open slightly, letting small amounts of water into your mouth. By purging the system and shaking it, you can usually clear out trapped particles. (Don't bang the mouthpiece against your hand—it's delicate.) If this doesn't work, terminate your dive until you can clear the valve.

The Buddy System

The importance of diving with a buddy cannot be emphasized too strongly; that's why it is mentioned often in this book. Some "loners" may derive great satisfaction from diving by themselves; however, they are completely at the mercy of a very fickle fate and are at a great disadvantage should the time come that they do need help.

The buddy system is the working together of two divers as a single unit. Buddies are constantly aware of each other, always at hand if needed. In the water, buddies should never be more than 6 to 10 feet apart and, if visibility is poor, the distance should be decreased, even to the point that the two swimmers are holding onto each other. In areas free of underwater entanglements, a length of rope can be held between buddies to maintain contact. The line can have a loop at each end to hold, but it should never be tied to either diver or looped around their wrists, in case it becomes caught on something.

If buddies lose sight of each other, and if a slow, 360-degree visual sweep, while looking up and down, doesn't reestablish contact, both should surface immediately.

Two divers together are better than three, because when three are down, there is a tendency for one to think that the other two can keep track of each other. Underwater and on the surface, buddies should move at the speed of the slower diver. Both should be thoroughly familiar with hand signals and ready to turn on a reserve valve if one partner signals that he is low on air. Whenever one diver has to go on reserve, both should surface, even though the other has plenty of air left.

Choose your buddy carefully and feel confidence in diving with this person because someday one of you may have to help the other in a real emergency.

Buddy Breathing

If a diver's air supply is exhausted in deep water, the emergency sharing of one air supply by two divers is necessary. The face-to-face method of buddy breathing, with the regulator being controlled by the right hand of the supplier, is preferred for either stationary breathing or vertical ascents.

With the left hand, each diver should take a firm hold on the other's right shoulder strap. The supplier should hold his regulator with his right hand, take two breaths, then move the regulator to his partner's mouth; the receiver can guide him lightly with his own right hand. The receiver takes two breaths and lets the supplier return the regulator to his own mouth. This trading and breathing should be done smoothly, with no fumbling and no grabbing. Close eye contact is important for reassurance to both divers.

If it is necessary to swim horizontally to get to shallower water, the

Buddy breathing calls for cooperation and coordination between two divers sharing a common air supply and one second stage. As the regulator is passed back and forth, each diver must exhale slightly so as not to build up excessive pressure in the lungs or develop the bad habit of holding the breath.

An octopus rig gives two divers separate second stages and thus allows both divers to continue breathing easily while ascending from depth. To ensure their keeping together, the diver sharing should hold onto the diver supplying.

supplier should swim on his right side and the receiver on his left. Between exchanges, the diver waiting for the air should look ahead to control direction. Both divers must monitor the air gauge of the one remaining tank because buddy breathing will generally deplete the air supply faster than one-man use will.

As soon as both divers feel calm, they should let all the air out of their vests and begin a controlled vertical ascent together, continuing to buddy breathe. It is imperative that during the ascent the diver waiting for air exhale to prevent an embolism.

Even more practicable than buddy breathing from a shared regulator is sharing one diver's air supply by using an octopus rig. When breathing from an octopus, swim at the supplier's side. Because the air in the tank will be used up fast with two people breathing it, breathe slowly and head for the surface right away.

Because this method is the easiest and safest to use in reaching the surface in an out-of-air situation, most national certifying agencies require student divers to have a secondary second stage during their initial open-water experience.

Emergency Swimming Ascent

As the name implies, an emergency swimming ascent is a means of getting to the surface in an emergency, most notably when your air supply is exhausted. This technique requires a great deal of practice under expert supervision.

Since this is an independent means of reaching the surface safely without air support, you must remain calm and retain a great deal of self confidence. First adjust your buoyancy, then tilt your head back, gently supporting your regulator in your mouth with your hand. Keeping the regulator in your mouth allows you to try for a breath as residual air in your tank expands. Start swimming toward the surface while continually exhaling. *Do not hold your breath.*

As you go up at about 60 feet per minute, look up, keeping your head tilted well back and your mouth relaxed so that expanding air in your lungs can escape. *Do not hold your breath* and don't try to force the air out. Just keep looking up, so your air passages stay straight and open, and allow the air to bubble out through your lips.

The first thought that usually occurs to a novice diver who has become proficient at surfacing while breathing on scuba is: "But I can't hold my breath that long!" The point is, you do not hold your breath at all but let it freely and naturally escape as you ascend. Emergency swimming ascents have been suc- cessfully made from depths well below 200 feet by experienced divers, and the average sport diver should be able to handle such ascents from 40 feet.

Emergency swimming ascent is an important diving technique. It should be practiced first in a swimming pool, where you travel horizontally to simulate depths greater than that of the pool's deep end. In open water you can ascend straight up. In either locale, however, never practice emergency swimming ascents without an instructor or an experienced buddy at hand.

As you gain confidence in your diving ability and your physical stamina increases, you'll be able to make emergency swimming ascents from greater depths. Always remember that fear and panic are the deciding factors that make you unable to handle stress.

Buoyant Ascent

A buoyant ascent should be used only as a last resort. If you feel weak, as though you might pass out before you can reach the surface on a normal ascent, inflate your vest and/or drop your weight belt. Because of the increased buoyancy, you will immediately head up. If wearing a wet suit, you'll accelerate even more rapidly as its air cells expand with reduced pressure. As you go up, bleed off expanding air in your vest and *do not hold your breath.* At the surface, if you are totally exhausted and breathing is difficult, ditch your weight belt if you haven't already done so.

Never Hold Your Breath

Keep in mind that with all ascents the more distressed and excited you become, the faster you're going to burn up your remaining air, whether it be in your tank or in your lungs. Whatever the situation, evaluate it quickly, then take action calmly and positively. Just remember that no crisis can be so hazardous as to cause you to hold your breath while ascending. If you hold your breath, you might as well stay down.

SPECIAL SCUBA SKILLS

The fundamentals of safe scuba diving have been covered in previous pages of this chapter. Learning those basics is essential to your safety and to the well-being of anyone you dive with. Certain other scuba techniques are not absolutely necessary to master, but they will make you a better diver by sharpening your skills, increasing your self-confidence, and giving you greater familiarity with your body and your equipment. The more at ease you can feel in the alien environment of the underwater, even though adorned with several pounds of rubber, metal, and plastic, the more you can enjoy yourself. And the better a diver you become, the less aware you are of your equipment. You simply and instinctively know what to do and when to do it, and every moment spent under the surface is a pleasurable one.

Ditch and Recovery

You will probably never have to ditch your gear, yet this is an excellent skill in equipment control. Its mastery will give you greater confidence in your diving gear and in your ability to handle it. Essentially, ditch and recovery is taking off everything except vest, wet suit, and swim suit, leaving it on the bottom while surfacing, and then descending to put it all on again. This skill is sometimes referred to as "doff and don."

While sitting or kneeling on the bottom in 10 to 20 feet of water, first remove your tank. You can do this by releasing the buckles and loosening the shoulder straps, then lifting the tank over your head or slipping out of the harness as if you were taking off a coat. Lay the tank down in front of you with the valve pointing toward you and the backpack up. Keep the regulator in your mouth so you can breathe, and be careful not to yank it out when you lay the tank down. With one hand holding the tank, remove your fins and secure them to one of the tank harness straps. Now stretch yourself out prone, facing the tank, remove your weight belt, and lay it over the tank. Remove your mask and wrap its strap around the tank valve. Next take a good breath, remove the regulator from your mouth, and turn off the air. Do not purge the regulator because doing so could break the watertight seal at the high-pressure seat. Last of all, make a good swimming ascent to the surface, exhaling all the way.

At the surface, relax for a moment before heading down. When you're ready, take several deep breaths but do not hyperventilate. Also, be careful not to overinflate your lungs, because that would affect your buoyancy on the bottom. Dive down, using the jackknife or pike dive to get below easily and quickly. At the bottom, lie flat, facing the valve end of your tank. Move the regulator to your mouth with your right hand and turn on the air with your left. Your first couple of breaths shouldn't be too deep, so that you don't start floating up. If you do start to rise, get your rear end and legs under you by sitting or kneeling on the bottom.

The order for putting on your equipment can vary, depending on what sequence feels most comfortable. One way is to sit, holding the tank between your thighs. Lay the weight belt across your lap, then put on the face mask and clear it. Slip on the fins. Now get into the tank harness by either the "jacket" or "overhead" method. With the tank firmly secured, lie on your stomach, put the weight belt across your back with the buckle in front, and secure it. Check all your equipment to make sure it is on right and properly fastened. Then make a normal ascent.

Equipment Exchange

Once you've mastered ditch and recovery, you are ready to tackle the more difficult equipment exchange. This skill brings into play all the other scuba skills you have learned: propulsion, buoyancy control, mask clearing, regulator clearing, and buddy breathing. It should be practiced over and over in a swimming pool before you attempt it in open water.

Two divers are needed; one wears fins, a mask and snorkel, tank and regulator, and weight belt; the other, just a swimsuit. Starting at one end of the deep part of the pool, both divers buddy breathe while swimming near the bottom to the other end. At that point, all equipment is transferred to the buddy and both divers buddy breathe back to the original starting point.

The sequence in which gear is transferred depends on personal preference and how well you and your partner work together. Remember that all during the second operation you must continue to buddy breathe, but not so deeply that either of you floats up.

One way is to first transfer the fins one at a time, with one diver always holding the other with a free hand. Next exchange the tank. Now the responsibility for sharing the air has shifted from one diver to the other. Transfer the mask, and, last of all, the weight belt. Check that everything is in order and head back to the starting point.

On the swim back, make sure that the diver supplying the air is on his right side and the receiver is on his left side.

Bail Off

A skill to be practiced only by the more advanced student or diver is the bail off ("bail out" in some diving circles).

Stand at the edge of the deep end of the pool, grasping in your hands your fins, mask with snorkel, tank with regulator attached (but air turned off), and weight belt. On the command "Go!" take a medium-deep breath and jump in. Unless you are wearing a wet suit you will sink quickly, so be prepared to equalize immediately. As soon as you hit the water, put the regulator in your mouth and turn on the air. Then, on the bottom, don all gear in a manner and order that demonstrate equipment control and self-control. At no time should anything be abandoned or laid loosely on the bottom.

For the novice diver, the bail off can be dangerous. Close supervision must be standard practice for a diver perfecting this skill.

DECOMPRESSION DIVES

No matter what the depth, some nitrogen is taken up by your body during every dive. The amount that goes into solution in the blood and tissues depends on the depth of the dive and on how long you are down (your bottom time). If the amount of body nitrogen exceeds a critical amount, your ascent must be delayed long enough for the excess to work its way out of the blood and tissues into the lungs and then be exhaled. If this *gradual* elimination of nitrogen is not allowed to take place—if your ascent is too rapid—decompression sickness, the bends, will follow.

A decompression stop is the specified amount of time a diver spends at a specified depth to allow residual nitrogen to pass out of his body. In the Appendix, you will find a series of tables giving decompression stops for various bottom times. Even if you never expect to make a decompression dive, you should understand how to use the tables.

Some divers have the mistaken notion that they don't have to worry about decompression, assuming that they can never exceed permissible no-decompression bottom time on only a single tank of air. This is a false assumption and it can get you into a lot of trouble if you subscribe to it. It is very possible to be bent on one tank.

Making decompression stops requires considerable planning. You must have extra air tanks available at predetermined depths. A safety diver—*not* your buddy—must often be ready to help at stops. Sometimes a surface attendant may be needed. You must have an accurate depth gauge and a good underwater watch, or else a reliable decompression meter.

What is a recompression chamber? It's a metal tank that can be pressurized. It will hold a diver and sometimes an attendant as well. Referred to as a "chamber of horrors," it is a cramped box, extremely hot and frightfully noisy when the pressure is raised. A patient must stay in it, at depth, for several hours, until all symptoms of the bends disappear.

Although many U.S. Navy and Coast Guard stations maintain recompression facilities and have qualified operators on duty, recompression treatment is no treat, and it is not free, even to taxpayers. A diver who has undergone recompression successfully and is feeling like his old self again may have a relapse when presented with a whopping bill for the service.

Decompression is a normal procedure for allowing residual nitrogen to pass out of a diver's body. *Re*compression is an emergency procedure for helping a diver who has been hit by the bends, who has not spent enough time at depth for excess nitrogen to leave his body. Recompression is, in effect, returning to depth to force residual nitrogen into solution in the body, then "coming up" gradually to allow the gas to leave the system. Actually taking a bent diver back into the water is not advisable, since submerging him may do more harm than good. Instead, a recompression chamber must be used.

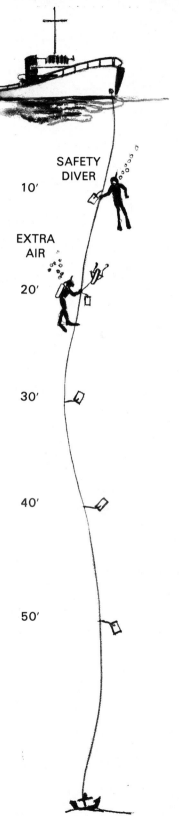

SAFETY DIVER

10′

EXTRA AIR

20′

30′

40′

50′

Decompression stops are necessary when you have exceeded the no-decompression limits (see Chapter 4 and tables in the Appendix) and must pause at certain depths to allow dissolved nitrogen to work its way out of your bloodstream to avoid the bends. Decompression must be planned well in advance of a dive and not be a spur-of-the-moment decision. Depending on the amount of decompression required, you may need marker tags at 10-foot intervals, extra air at certain stations, and a safety diver to assist in changing tanks.

Diver hand signals are an accepted means of communicating at the surface or underwater. Because signals may differ slightly in different geographical areas, make sure you and your buddy agree on them before starting a dive.

A. "I'm low on air." Fist is held to chest.
B. "I'm going on reserve air supply." Fist is held to forehead.
C. "I'm out of air." Flat hand makes throat-slitting motion.

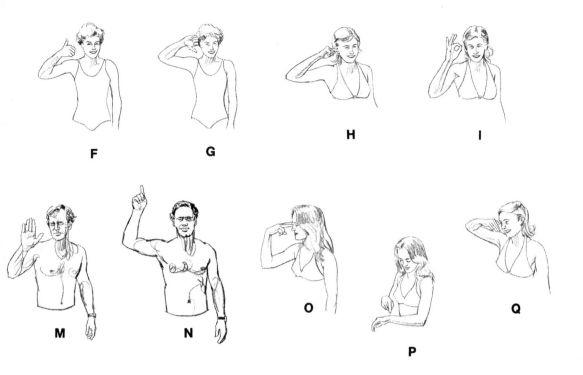

F

G

H

I

M

N

O

P

Q

D. "I want to buddy breathe." Fingers tap mouth.
E. "I need help." Hands make choking motion at neck.
F. "I'm going up." Thumb points up.
G. "I'm going down." Thumb points down.
H. "I can't equalize." Forefinger points to ear.
I. "Everything is okay." Thumb and forefinger form a circle.
J. "Everything is so-so." Hands turn palms up, then palms down, or, in response to another hand signal, "I don't know."
K. "I'm cold." Hands hug body.
L. "Wait here." Fists face out, at head height.
M. "Stop." Hand is held open, palm out, at head height.
N. "Assemble here." Forefinger points up, makes circular motion.
O. "Look at what I'm going to point to." First and second fingers point to eyes.
P. "Look at that." Forefinger points to something.
Q. "Start swimming." Flat hand, palm down, makes swimming motion in front of face.
R. "Let's go that way." Forefinger points to a direction in front of face.
S. "I need help." Arm waves up and down, at surface.
T. "I have a cramp." Fist hits open palm of hand.

HOW MUCH AIR DO YOU CONSUME?

Everyone breathes at a different rate. Some divers burn up a tank of air in a very short time; others seem to use hardly any at all. With experience and practice, most divers can improve their air consumption rate by learning to relax, by moving efficiently through the water, and by breathing easily. The amount of air you use per minute is important to know when you team up with a buddy, and invaluable to know when you plan dives beyond "no-decompression" limits.

In the following table, keep calculations simple by using a relatively shallow test depth, say 20 feet, and a fairly short test time, such as 10 minutes. The figure on Line H, your air consumption in pounds per minute per atmosphere, should be entered on a strip of marking tape and attached to the side of your submersible pressure gauge for ready reference.

Diver's name_____Date_____

A. Test depth: ____ feet.

B. Test time: ____ minutes.

C. Cylinder pressure at start of dive: ____ PSIG (pounds per square inch gauge).

D. Cylinder pressure at finish of dive: ____ PSIG.

E. Subtract Line D from Line C: ____ PSIG. (This figure represents air used during test dive.)

F. Divide Line E by Line B: $\frac{E}{B}$ = ____ lbs/min. (This figure represents pounds of air consumed per minute at the test depth.)

G. Test depth in atmospheres: ____ ATM (Atmospheres).
Example: For a depth of 20 feet, test depth = $\frac{33 + 20 \text{ ATM}}{33}$

H. Divide Line F by Line G: $\frac{F}{G}$ = ____ lbs/min/ATM. (This figure is your air consumption in pounds per minute per atmosphere.)

Example: If the answer on Line H was 25 lbs/min/ATM, you would consume:

    25 lbs/min at the surface
    50 lbs/min at 33 feet
    75 lbs/min at 66 feet
    100 lbs/min at 99 feet

7

The Ways the Ocean Behaves

Where and When to Dive

For a long time divers have been making excursions into the upper layers of the ocean, but such trips have hardly penetrated the seas and have lasted for relatively brief periods. Only within the present generation have human beings really begun to explore the depths, putting forth a concentrated effort to not just visit the underwater world and marvel at its strangeness, but to adapt themselves to the ocean as a total environment.

The earth is almost three-fourths ocean, amounting to more than 300 million cubic miles of water. There is obviously a lot of this environment to learn about. Though the moods and movements of this once mysterious surrounding are slowly being understood, they still differ from anything we have experienced on dry land, and the unwritten rules for staying healthy in one place simply don't apply to the other. Because the ocean has its own rule book, it requires of even the sport diver a basic knowledge of its weather, its tides, its waves, and its currents.

For example, being familiar with ways that changing weather conditions affect the water where you dive can save you a great deal of time, maybe even a little trouble. Few things are as

153

annoying as driving many miles and hiking a considerable distance to a diving site, lugging tanks and other paraphernalia, and then finding the water so rough or so stirred up that a dive is out of the question. And few things are so discouraging as making a reasonably good entry, then wishing you'd never gotten into the water because a rising wind, an offshore current, and thundering surf all conspire to prevent you from ever getting home again.

WHAT ARE TIDES?

Tidal movement is the regular rise and fall of water along the seacoast. It is caused by the combined gravitational attraction of the sun and moon, which actually pulls the earth's waters in certain directions. When the earth, the moon, and the sun are all in a straight line, the pull is greatest on that side of the earth, causing a spring tide. (The term "spring" has nothing to do with the season of the year; it refers to "springing up" of the waters.) At the same time on the opposite side of the earth, away from the sun and moon, the spring tide is lowest because the waters are pulled away from that point. Spring tides occur at full and new moon. Near the first and third quarters of the moon, when sun and moon pull at right angles to each other, a neap (or "nipped") tide occurs.

Depending on the topography of the ocean bottom and the configuration of the coast, tides may rise and fall as little as 1 foot at a mid-ocean island, such as Tahiti, or vary as much as 40 feet, as they do in New Brunswick's Bay of Fundy. (At the South Pole there is no tide at all.) In most coastal regions a full tidal cycle from high to low to high occurs every twenty-four hours.

The wise diver will study tide tables, usually available at dive shops and sporting goods stores, and will try to plan excursions for slack periods between tide changes. Swimming or diving as the water is moving in toward shore (flooding) or out away from shore (ebbing) can sometimes be a trial if you have to struggle against tidal currents to get to where you want to go. During ebb and flood tides, the strong horizontal flow of water will affect your starting point and termination point. You may enter the water at one place and shortly thereafter find yourself hundreds of yards downstream or upstream without having swum there. Tidal currents can be used for a free ride, but taking advantage of them requires a thorough knowledge of how they run in a particular area.

Generally speaking, along most sandy coasts the best visibility is during high tide, whereas low tides tend to stir up the bottom and drag debris off the beachfront into the water. If you're uncertain of the tidal character of an area, be sure to ask local divers about its peculiarities.

WHAT ARE WAVES?

Waves are a series of more or less regular transfers of energy within water—a rather stuffy way of saying that wave water doesn't move but wave energy does. As waves travel along the surface of a body of water, there is actually very little lateral movement of the water, the physical motion being mostly an up-and-down action. Assisted by wind, waves travel for hundreds of miles, but the actual water stays pretty much in the same place.

Waves are caused by wind that pushes the surface of the water into wrinkles, by tidal forces (tides are actually long waves), by currents, by high- and low-pressure atmospheric conditions, and by earthquakes or movements of the ocean bottom. Such major earth shifts often create monstrous waves properly known as tsunamis, which are sometimes—though improperly—called tidal waves even though they are not caused by tides.

Waves generated far out at sea may arrive at a coastal area in the form of long, large swells that pound onto a beach as magnificent surf. Surf is lovely to watch and fun to play in (wearing just a wet suit for buoyancy, let yourself be tossed around—the experience will build self-confidence), but it is no good for diving. The water movements are too violent, and visibility is close to zero where the water is spilling over and rushing about. You must get out past the surf line to where the surface is steadier and the water movement at the bottom is calmer.

Wave-watching for even a few minutes is intriguing because you can quickly learn a great deal about the ocean bottom in the area by seeing how the waves behave. At a shallow beach, where the bottom deepens very gradually, surf will break a good distance out and roll in toward the shore steadily. Where the bottom drops off sharply, forming a steep beach, the surf line will be closer to shore. If you see lines of waves breaking far out, then leveling off, then breaking again closer in, you can be sure that there is a reef or shoal at just about the location of the first wave break. If you spot an isolated patch of white water that foams and displays an area of miniature surf on the inrush of waves, it indicates a rock with its top close to the surface.

Swell and surf may exist even if there are no local winds, the waves having begun many miles out at sea. However, if a stiff breeze is blowing in a coastal area, large waves may become unstable and start spilling over far behind the normal surf line, developing what is referred to as chop. Chop may be somewhat of a trial for surface swimming because water tends to spill into the open end of a snorkel unexpectedly and frequently. But chop is only a surface condition, and usually just a few feet down the water is fairly calm.

Often chop, swell, surf, wind waves, and currents get all mixed together, and the result is called a confused area of water. The term is appropriate, because figuring out how the water is moving in such an area is nearly impossible. In studying the water prior to a dive, be on the lookout for a place in which the surface surges, runs, and spills wildly in an irregular way and stay clear of it. This is not good diving territory, and it can be dangerous.

Fighting your way through crashing waves may represent a challenge to you, a kind of personal proving ground. But be sure you know your limitations and respect them. Don't use all your energy going in one direction only to learn that you haven't enough strength to get back. Also, respect your buddy's capabilities. Your buddy may not be as gung ho as you.

WHAT ARE CURRENTS?

Remember that wave action is a transfer of energy, usually in an up-and-down motion, with very little sideways water movement. Currents, however, are actual horizontal movements of water. Because currents are the flow of water from one place to another, they can move objects—such as a float or a diver —considerable distances. Currents can be a nuisance if you try to swim against them or a great help if you swim in the same direction they are moving. You can't ignore their existence because sometime you're going to find yourself in one.

Undertow

The most common current on an ocean beach is undertow, the rushing return of water seaward underneath the wave action that brought it to the beach. Wherever water slides far up the beach and then rushes back, you can be sure that there is a healthy undertow. If no waves are breaking or washing up, there won't be an undertow.

Undertow, or backwash, is usually not a dangerous current, except perhaps to small children playing in the shallows. Despite all the horror stories, it's not something that's going to grab you, suck you down, and drag you out to sea, since it flows only to the surf line, where it dissipates. If you feel "caught" by undertow and imagine that it is pulling you inexorably away from land, just hold your breath, swim along with the current, and enjoy the short ride. In a couple of seconds you'll be in or beyond the surf line and can turn around and catch a wave going back up the beach.

When making a beach entry, you should let undertow work for you.

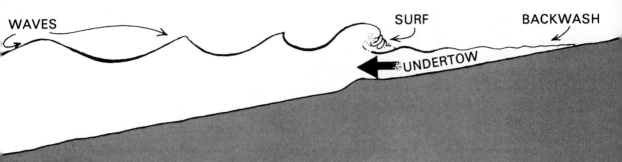

WAVES　　　　　　　　**SURF**　　　**BACKWASH**

UNDERTOW

Undertow is not a regular current but a seaward flow of water that has been carried up a beach slope by wave action, as is shown in this side view along a beach. The locale of undertows and their strength can vary from day to day, even from hour to hour, depending on tides and surf conditions. Undertow is not dangerous as long as you know how to handle yourself in the water.

Wade out until the water is about up to your knees, keeping your legs bent so a wave won't knock you over and the backwash won't pull your feet out from under you. Just after a breaking wave, when water is flowing strongly seaward, dive deep and swim with the current, letting it carry you along the bottom to calmer waters past the surf.

Rip Currents

A rip current (sometimes erroneously called riptide) is a more serious phenomenon. It is caused by water's being pushed by wave action between a bar or a reef and the shore, then rushing back seaward through a low spot or a channel in the bar or reef. It is a strong flow of water out through the surf zone, and it can definitely be dangerous if you don't know how to cope with it. It travels with greater force and for a longer distance than undertow. If you find yourself unwillingly in a rip—or in any kind of current, for that matter—remember to relax. Remain calm and swim with the flow until you're free of it, then return to the beach to one side of the rip.

Rip currents can usually be detected from the beach. The higher you can get to look down on the water, the better you can see them. Watch for a gap in the line of breakers, usually accompanied by an area of turbulence closer in. This rough, broken area inshore is where the piled-up water is beginning to flow back out. Also look for a channel of dirty water perpendicular to the shoreline, as rips tend to carry sand and other particles out with them. Note that the center of the rip channel is marked by waves lower than those on the sides.

If you see several rips of varying size, try to spot them relative to landmarks that will be visible from the water. That way you can later relocate the areas when you're exiting and avoid them.

Experienced divers often utilize rip currents to get out from the beach fast. It's another free ride, but it shouldn't be attempted by a novice who hasn't yet gained good experience in handling himself and his equipment in surf and undertow. To ride a rip, put a little air into your buoyancy compensator vest and wade into the water directly opposite the break in the waves where the current is flowing out. As soon as you feel a pulling seaward, relax and swim

Rip currents are formed when water piles up behind a sandbar or a reef, then rushes out to sea through a low spot, as is shown in this bird's-eye view looking down on a beach. Rips travel out beyond the surf line, so if you purposely take a free ride on one, or find yourself an unwilling passenger, stay with it to the dispersal area, then swim off to one side of the main channel.

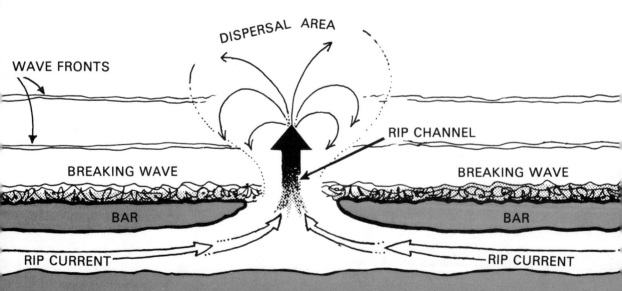

DISPERSAL AREA

WAVE FRONTS

RIP CHANNEL

BREAKING WAVE   BREAKING WAVE

BAR   BAR

RIP CURRENT   RIP CURRENT

BEACH

easily along with the current on the surface. Let it carry you until you're free of it in deep water, then head for your diving grounds. Don't expect to dive in the dispersal area just beyond the breaker zone where the rip breaks up because underwater visibility there is nil. If you have to exit in that area, don't attempt to swim against the rip channel but return well to one side of the outgoing flow.

Thermoclines

If you have ever been swimming in a sun-warmed lake and have dived down a few feet into shockingly cold water, you know what a thermocline is. One of the most unusual phenomena to be found in the ocean, as well as in quarries, lakes, and rivers, thermoclines are sharply changing temperature gradients occurring at varying depths. Though not currents, they may rise and fall, changing levels several times over a period of twenty-four hours, and their presence is felt only when you enter one. So sharply defined are thermoclines that it's possible to have the upper part of your body in water of a comfortable temperature and your legs and feet in a chilling cold layer.

When thermoclines are known to exist at a diving site, they should be taken into consideration in dive planning. Exposure to sudden and extreme changes in temperature when you aren't prepared for them can result in cramps, fatigue, and greater air consumption.

WHERE THE WATER MEETS THE LAND

From the rugged shores of Washington to the sweeping beaches of Florida, from the submarine canyons of California to the shallows of the Carolinas, coastline conditions vary tremendously. Each bit of ocean edge, each strip of shore, has its own special character insofar as diving is concerned, and getting in and out of the ocean safely calls for special skills and a degree of knowledge not required of the casual, fun-in-the-sun swimmer.

As well-trained and experienced as a West Coast diver may be, for example, he has no idea of the moods and behavior of the Atlantic along the New England shore. Novice divers have gotten into quick trouble by assuming that all water everywhere behaves the same, and even experienced divers have had bad experiences when they allowed themselves to believe that the ocean holds no surprises. The best source of information for any area is a local diver.

Certain characteristics of water movement *can* be recognized by reading the surf, which means checking out the diving area and using your knowledge to interpret coastal conditions bearing on your safety. It means walking up and down the beach, studying the lay of the land and the movements of the water and figuring out what's happening before you put on your face mask or fins. It means remaining ever watchful while entering, while in the water, and while exiting, being prepared for anything.

Start by acquiring a set of tide tables or checking tide times in the daily newspapers. Diving in slack water assures the easiest entry—at least from the standpoint of tides. But remember that this period lasts for only about half an hour before flood or ebb tide starts moving the waters again. Of course, tidal conditions may change even while you're reading the surf or are in the water, so be ready for this eventuality.

When planning a dive, check the weather report twenty-four hours ahead. If a storm is expected, be prepared to scrub the trip, but don't give up if the bad weather is still a good way off. Sometimes a calm preceding a storm offers excellent diving. Just don't cut it so close that you are caught in the water when the wind rises. Right after a storm or heavy rain the diving usually is not good. The bottom is too roiled, or runoff from the land makes the water so dirty that you can't see anything past the end of your nose. Again, to save yourself time, ask about water conditions at local dive shops. Usually there'll be someone around who has just come back from "Old-Such-and-So-Cove" and will fill you in on conditions there.

At the beach, while you are trying to decide if conditions are good enough to permit a dive, remember that waves generate terrific force and that you are pretty much at their mercy. Don't go attacking waves that give you that sinking feeling in the pit of your stomach. Try to determine the direction of any currents so you can take advantage of them. Check especially for rip currents by getting as high above the water as you can to look for a break in the smooth wave fronts.

Check for water clarity by studying wave fronts just before they break. Clear blue colors indicate good visibility. Faded colors and water with loose particles of marine growth indicate poor visibility and a turned-up bottom. Watch wave action to learn the timing of the waves. If a wind is building up, as is common late in the afternoon along some coastal areas, bigger waves and decreasing underwater visibility are sure to follow.

The following sections discuss several typical coastal configurations and illustrate their water movements. In the drawings, currents are indicated by

Steep Beaches

One of the most difficult entries is from a sharply sloped beach where the water is breaking high up, washing hard against a berm (steep bank), then flowing seaward with great velocity. An entry here should be attempted only by very strong swimmers and experienced divers. You must watch for a series of low waves, get into them fast, dive deep, and swim out hard to escape dumping surf. Even then, onrushing water may sweep you up the face of the beach and the outflow will drag you back, rolling you all over the place. If you get knocked down, don't attempt to stand up. Instead, roll over, face down, and either crawl into and under the next wave or crawl up onto the beach.

Under such rough conditions, your swim fins must be well secured on your feet, and you should keep one hand on your face mask. Getting through a rough-and-tumble surf only to discover you're missing a fin can be most disheartening.

Sandy Beaches with Bars

Clean, even sandy beaches with mirror-smooth waters or low surf are the diver's dream. All you have to do is walk out and swim away, as described in Chapter 5 under Beach Entry. However, nature does not always provide ideal diving conditions, and, more often than not, a sandy beach will have an offshore bank or shoal that does all sorts of tricky things with the water. Bars are a common condition along the beaches of the New England states and in areas where heavy surf carries sand from the beach and deposits it offshore. Generally, strong rip currents will be flowing out between bars, and entries should be made close to their edges. Exit over (not around) a bar and on into the calmer waters between it and the beach.

When you are exiting over a shoal and feel bottom just a couple of feet below you, don't be fooled into thinking you're on the beach. Weary divers have been known to stand up, remove their fins and mask, and proceed to walk the rest of the way in, only to drop unexpectedly into water well over their heads on the lee side of the bank.

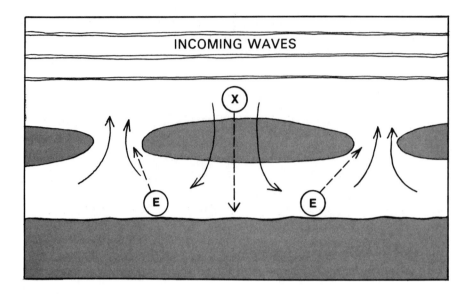

A sandy beach with bars may have rip currents flowing out between the bars. Best entries (E) are made close to the edges of the bars; exits (X) should be made over a bar to the calm water between it and the beach.

Exposed Points

Exposed points of land bear the brunt of incoming seas, which eventually wear them away, blending them into the beach on either side. Waves usually approach a point at an angle, and the roughest spots are those that take the full force of the moving water. Whenever possible, it's best to enter and exit from the protected side, where waves are slowed to a relative calm in the "shadow" of the point. If you must enter on the windward side, keep as far up the beach as possible, away from the point, to avoid being washed into it. And if you must exit on a point's exposed flank, expect rough water.

Rocky Beaches

When entering over rocks or coral in shallow water, wade in cautiously, being careful not to trip and fall. As soon as you can, lie down and use shallow kicks

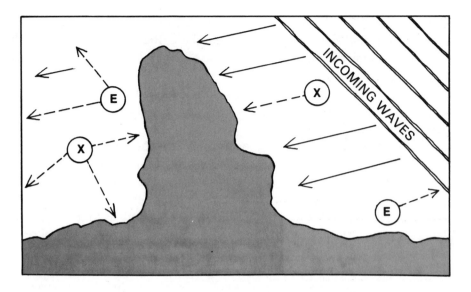

Exposed points cause convergence of wave energy, and the action is rougher for divers entering the water on the exposed flank. Best entries (E) are immediately behind the point, or far down the beach in front of it. The best exits (X) are in the protected cove behind the point, though a skilled diver used to rough water could come in on the exposed flank.

to swim out with seaward-flowing water. Hold on to protruding rocks or marine vegetation to prevent being washed toward shore with incoming waves or surge, and swim along with the backwash carrying you deeper. To protect your head and face from rocks hiding just below the surface, keep one hand extended.

Exiting over rocks calls for care because you'll be behind the breakers and won't be able to see over the surface. Thus, about the same time you find yourself in a trough, rising waves will cover shallow rocks ahead of you. Study the shore from behind the surf line and try to exit along a stretch where waves seem to be smallest and there is a minimum of white water. Remember to ride along with the ingoing surge and hang on against the backwash. When surge takes you between or over rocks, be alert for its reversing direction or dissipating and leaving you high but not so dry, or laying you on a bed of sea urchins.

At a very rugged shore where there are no shallows for wading, walk out over the rocks to a big one where waves rise up but don't wash over the rock. Carry your fins and mask until you get there, then don them. Watch the wave action and look for a couple of big ones. After one big wave hits and starts to settle back, throw your float far out so it will be carried beyond the breakers. Then on the next large outsurge, when the water is again at its highest and just starting out, jump in, using a giant stride entry, and quickly swim out on the surface to your float.

To exit from such an area, choose a rock with good handholds, one that does not get completely washed over with waves and that is connected to shore, not isolated like an island. Approach it cautiously so you're not thrown against it suddenly, and guard against swirling currents that take you where you don't want to go. As the surge rises, swim hard to the rock, climb as high as you can, and hang on against the backwash. On the next surge, climb higher out of reach of the waves.

Rather than attempting to ride an inner tube or a surf mat in when exiting over rocks, keep one end of the float line in your hand and retrieve it only after you are safely out of the water.

Rocky Coves with Reefs

A rocky or a coral reef causes water to behave much as it does when passing over a sandbar. Currents are generated that flow seaward around the ends of the reef with great velocity. Entering near these ends (with care) will let you swim out with the current, and exiting far to either side is the safest bet. Exit directly over the reef only with care, and time your movements with the wave action to avoid getting scraped.

Deep Coves with Shallow Bottoms

In a deep cove with a shallow bottom, the bottom causes waves to slow down and converge on the cove edges, where they break as heavy surf, whereas in the center the surf is more gentle. However, the convergence and divergence of force may concentrate energy in the center, causing a powerful, seaward-flowing current there.

Although the best entry is at the place with the least surf, in the center of the cove, be prepared to ride a rip out. Don't attempt to exit in the same place—you'll only be fighting against the current—but exit to one side or the other, prepared for surf. If you feel the flow moving you to the center, don't swim squarely across it but angle your way toward shore, letting drift carry you along as you close in on the beach.

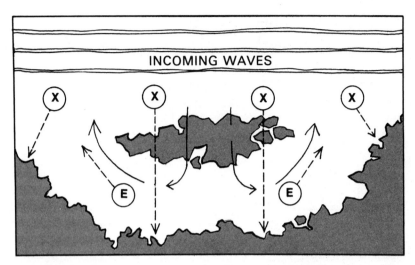

A rocky cove with an offshore reef has water action much like that depicted for exposed points. Seaward currents rushing around the ends of the reef make these areas good entry points (E), but be sure to stay clear of rocks or coral if you ride the currents out. Make exits (X) over the reef, or else far to either side to avoid the outward bound currents.

A deep cove with a shallow bottom is characterized by gentle surf in the center, which is the best locale for entry (E). However, there may also be an outflow, so be prepared for some current when entering. Make your exit (X) well to either side of the center.

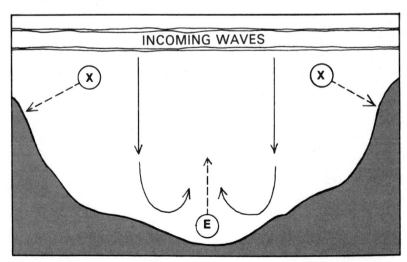

Deep Coves with Submarine Canyons

Water movements from wave action in both a deep cove fronted by a submarine canyon and a shallow cove with a deep bottom are similar. Convergence takes place on the sides, and there may be a center outflow. In addition, the combination of wave convergence and energy generation from deep in the canyon will cause huge surf along the sides and lesser surf in the center. Entering along the edges is safest, and exiting should be done far to the side, out of the heavy surf area.

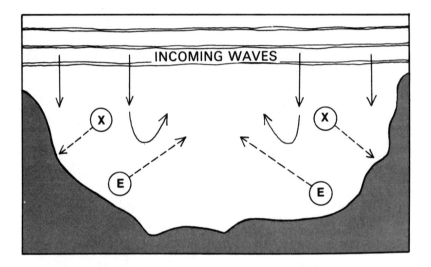

A submarine canyon fronting a deep cove creates wave convergence on the sides with resulting high surf in those areas. Plan entries (E) toward the central portion of the cove, where wave action tends to be less, and exit (X) far up on the sides, out of the heavy surf.

8

Life Beneath the Surface

Inhabitants of the Marine World

Oceanography is the study of chemical, physical, and biological interrelationships in the sea. Among its many facets are the varied ways that plants and animals live and protect themselves in order to survive. A detailed treatment of oceanic life is beyond the scope of this book and would be of little use to the sport diver; however, a look at a few of the forms of sea life—especially those that you are likely to come in contact with —will acquaint you with their unusual survival tactics and defense mechanisms, some of which you may at some time meet firsthand.

Man's relations with the sea reach far back to prehistoric times when shore dwellers simply waded along the rocks to gather shellfish for food. As man developed into a tool-using creature, he learned to spear fish in the shallows and later to cast crude nets into deeper waters. Then as he took to ships, he began to harvest seagoing life rather than simply hunting it.

Of course, the sea and its bounty were not made solely for mankind. The oceans were a prolific broth of interrelated nutrients, plants, and animals long before humans existed. A "big three" group of chemicals—the phosphates, the nitrates, the silicates—forms a nutritive base that has sup-

167

ported an incredibly huge population of single-celled, free-floating aquatic plants—the phytoplankton—for hundreds of millions of years. These tiny plants in turn support large numbers of small animals ranging from microscopic protozoa to larval fishes—the zooplankton.

Drifting and floating at the will of current and wave, both kinds of plankton together are fed upon by crustaceans and small fishes, which support larger fishes, marine mammals, and finally man. This relation is commonly referred to as the food pyramid of the sea, and man is frequently depicted at the top of the pyramid, a sort of king of the hill, on which nothing else feeds.

But we human beings retain this dominant role only as long as we are aware of what is going on around us in the underwater world and appreciate our position as latecomers. Certainly the day will arrive when we will move about the depths almost as freely as we do on land, and the ocean will no longer hold mystery or hazard for us. But as an educational step toward that day it behooves us to respect the sea's unique life forms and learn to coexist with them.

MARINE PLANT LIFE

Perhaps the most common plants found in either salt water or fresh water are the algae. These include the seaweeds, the kelps, the pond scums, and several other chlorophyll-bearing plants that grow in the water or at the water's edge. Most algae exist in relatively shallow places, clinging securely to rocks and other outcroppings. Varied forms of green and brown algae grow on intertidal rocks as slimes or slippery weeds, much as moss grows on a shaded tree trunk. Deriving nourishment from water and from the sun's rays, algae is a chief source of food as well as shelter for countless marine creatures. Small fish and shellfish are permanent residents of algae habitats, never straying far from their protective home. As innocuous as these plants usually are to a diver, they can be treacherous underfoot. Divers should exercise caution when entering or exiting over weed-grown rocks, which can be as slippery as oil.

Giant kelp—another form of algae—is the forest of the ocean, attaining lengths of as much as 100 feet and growing at an amazing rate of 12 to 24 inches a day. Unlike a tree—its dry land counterpart—kelp does not grow from the soil or sand of the bottom but anchors itself to rocks with a tight network of exposed "roots" called a holdfast. The holdfast usually does its job well, as can be seen underwater when surges and currents pull the plants first in one direction, then in another. During violent storms, though, kelp stalks are often snapped or the holdfast is torn loose and the plants drift free, eventually washing up on the beach. You've probably come across the whiplike stalks and 169 the ball-shaped air bladders that pop when you step on them.

Diving in and under kelp is an experience unparalleled by other forms of exploration. Near the bottom the stalks rise majestically, almost as sturdy as palm trees. Branching and forking on their way up, the plants spread out into a thick canopy at the surface. The stalks of a kelp forest offer little difficulty to you as a diver. However, avoid patches of kelp at the surface if you can, because moving through the canopy can be tiring, especially if you're dressed in full scuba gear and towing a float or a game bag. There is no quick way through a kelp bed, but there are two swimming strokes that are fairly efficient as long as you take your time and don't let getting tangled upset you.

The kelp crawl is a kind of Australian crawl done in slow motion. Starting in a horizontal position with your arms close to your sides, raise one arm, reach out in front, lay it flat on the kelp, and press down while using the flutter kick. Repeat with the other arm. The idea is not to pull yourself forward, as in normal swimming, but to propel yourself by finning while using your hands and arms to press the kelp down momentarily as you pass over it. This stroke works well in a very heavy bed.

If surface growth is patchy or thin, you can usually make a path by parting the kelp with your hands and arms in a breast stroke action while propelling yourself with a flutter kick. Don't try to swim on your back or side through a kelp bed when wearing an air tank. You'll snag the valve assembly right away. Should you really get tangled at the surface, don't panic; you are not going to be dragged under. Make sure your flotation vest is inflated, then calmly think things out. Have your buddy aid in pulling free the stems, or use your knife to cut yourself loose. Keep calm and don't hurry or you may get yourself wound up all the more.

You can always take the shortest route out of a kelp canopy by pushing outward with your hands to make a "hole" and then dropping straight down, feet first. Just below the surface you can easily thread your way between the stalks to a clear spot or to the edge of the bed.

Surfacing in kelp should also be done in an unhurried, deliberate manner. Take your time as you rise, looking up to pick a clearing in the canopy where you see light. As you come up, keep both arms outstretched over your head so you can part the canopy and enlarge the opening.

The very thought of swimming in a kelp bed gives some people a creepy, distasteful feeling. This is a perfectly natural reaction since few persons are used to the kind of pressing-in sensation caused by smooth, clinging stems and fronds. Usually one or two "weed dives" are all it takes to make a confirmed kelp explorer out of even the most timid soul.

WATCH WHERE YOU WALK

When you make an entry or an exit in an area that receives a good deal of use by people, be especially wary of where you place your feet. Nature's hazards are relatively few compared with those created by civilization. Glass, pieces of metal, and other carelessly discarded bits of sharp-edged material lurk in beach sands and on shallow bottoms waiting for an unsuspecting diver to put a foot down in the wrong place. Even in deep water, broken bottles tossed overboard or washed out from the shallows may become wedged in rocks where they can lacerate flesh and tear wet suits.

Coral Cuts

Coral is actually a collection of skeletons from tiny, jellylike animals called coelenterates, a group including sea anemones, hydras, and jellyfish. Great masses of these skeletons form reefs and islands, chiefly in tropical waters and only above certain depths. Some coral is smooth, but most is as abrasive as a wood rasp. Therefore, never attempt to walk on coral in bare feet or wearing fins. If you fall, you'll lose a good deal of skin as well as dignity.

Cuts and scratches from coral may become infectious, and they can take a long time to heal. When you dive in coral waters, your best protection is some kind of clothing, such as long pants, a sweat shirt, or a wet suit. Cloth gloves will keep your hands from being nicked if you have to reach into a coral formation or push yourself away from one.

If you get a coral cut, clean the wound right away with plenty of soap and fresh water, making sure to remove any particles that may have embedded themselves under the skin. Then treat with a germicide ointment or powder. Some parts of the world—Florida, the West Indies, the Red Sea, the Southwest Pacific—are known for "stinging" or "fire" corals, which are not true corals but hydrozoans. Small pink or violet staghorn branches attract the eye of collectors, but one brush against them produces a burning rash that lasts for days.

Cone Shell Stings

Cone shells are a large family of cone-shaped snails, valued highly by collectors for their beautiful markings and colors. Cone shells inhabit mostly tropical waters of the Pacific, where they hide under coral heads or burrow across sandy bottoms, often leaving a trail as they move along. Cone shells live in the shallows, as well as in deeper waters, well within reach of both snorkelers and scuba divers.

Despite their beauty, cone shells defend themselves with a sharp, poison-filled structure that is employed like a dart or harpoon and that can inflict serious wounds. When handling a cone shell, wear heavy gloves and use a pair of tongs to grasp it by its broadest end. If the "mouth" should extend, drop the shell immediately. Because the dart can penetrate cloth, it's not a good idea to carry cone shells in even a fine-mesh game bag attached to your belt.

A stab wound may be as painful as a wasp sting, and some varieties of cone shells are poisonous enough to cause paralysis and heart failure. Recommended treatment includes lancing of the wound and removal of the venom by suction and bleeding. One cone shell, *Conus californicus,* inhabits the coastal waters of California but is not venomous.

Sea Urchin Punctures

Urchins are the porcupines of the ocean floor. Found in temperate sea waters all over the world, they range in size from juniors as small as a marble to giants 8 or 9 inches in diameter. They live in intertidal crevices, on the open ocean floor, attached to rocks, and even buried in small holes. Deep-water urchins often carpet large areas of the sea bottom.

An urchin looks like an overloaded pincushion with all the points facing out. The spines are sharp and brittle, and merely bumping them may cause them to be embedded and break off in your flesh. A puncture results in a burning pain, followed by inflammation and sometimes swelling.

Spines should be removed as soon as possible with a sterile needle and tweezers. Very deep punctures or resulting infections should receive medical attention.

When diving in unfamiliar waters, check for urchins before you start walking blindly into the water. During an exit, currents or surges can throw you into a whole colony of urchins, so be on your guard.

MARINE MAMMALS

Harmless air-breathing mammals that inhabit shallow coastal waters, sea lions and seals may frolic around a diver, nudging or occasionally nibbling at a fin in apparent play. Once in a while they may brush too close in their enthusiasm and knock a face mask or a regulator awry, though none of the action seems to be malicious. Still, many a diver has had an anxious moment when the dark shape of a sea lion zoomed past underwater, moving so fast he was positive it was a shark. Generally these creatures will stay clear of you unless you spear a fish in their territory, at which time it becomes fair game and the sea lion is usually the victor. Or a bull might mistake you for another male and feel you're a threat to his harem (sea lions are a bit nearsighted).

Sea otters are inquisitive and often come close to a diver to look him over, but they will usually stay just out of reach. Mother otters can be very protective of their pups and may nip at a diver to discourage any advances, so don't try to pet one, no matter how cute it looks.

The much maligned killer whale is a toothed whale related to the dolphins, growing in excess of 25 feet in length. It is identified by a thick, black body with prominent white markings, a high dorsal fin, and a large mouth containing many teeth. Killer whales are not the villainous man-eaters they were once thought to be, but they do attack schools of fish or marine mammals that frequent kelp beds and may not take the time to distinguish a diver from a seal.

HAZARDOUS ANIMAL LIFE

When you enter the underwater world, you are venturing into an environment very different from the one you have lived in all your life. Its inhabitants are no more used to you than you are to them. Over millions of years, some animals have evolved rather exotic means of self-protection and food gathering, and others may exhibit downright hostile attitudes when defending their own homes.

Jellyfish, Portuguese Man-of-War

Almost poetic in its free-drifting pulsations, the graceful jellyfish can be a real annoyance to divers who come in contact with them. Belonging to the coelenterate family, whose members are actually colonies of specialized organisms making up what appears to be a single individual, the semitransparent jellyfish has a body anywhere from 2 to 9 inches across, shaped somewhat like a rounded lampshade with fringes hanging from it. In these fringes, more properly called tentacles, are great numbers of nematocysts, sometimes referred to as "stinging cells." The nematocysts stun or kill small prey. However, jellyfish are not partial; their stinging is involuntary, and a diver whose skin is touched by one is likely to be seared as with a red-hot iron.

Another member of the same family, the Portuguese man-of-war, appears to be a harmless purple or pink sac, 3 to 12 inches long, filled with air. But dangling below the sac, or sail, are tentacles that may be as long as 90 feet in some Atlantic species, 30 to 40 feet in Pacific species. Being transparent, the tentacles are almost invisible underwater, and, like those of the jellyfish, can inflict serious stings. A brush with a tentacle may produce only a prickling sensation or it may raise great welts accompanied by an intense burning pain. People who are extrasensitive may become unconscious and experience breathing difficulties.

In treating jellyfish or Portuguese man-of-war stings, first remove any adhering tentacles by pulling them off. Some divers recommend wiping them off gently with sand, clothing, or a towel. Pour salt water on the area of the sting, then flood it with rubbing alcohol or household ammonia. Sprinkling meat tenderizer over the area helps to relieve pain. As soon as possible, obtain medical care.

The deadly sea wasp is similar in appearance to the Portuguese man-of-war with a nearly transparent bell-like body and tentacles 12 to 15 feet long. Sea wasp encounters have been known to cause death in a matter of minutes when immediate medical help was not forthcoming. Some authorities recommend administration of antivenin.

The jellyfish has been described as a stomach topped by a mouth surrounded by tentacles. Not true fish despite the name, these free-drifting creatures move through the water by contracting and relaxing their umbrella-shaped bodies. A watchful diver can steer clear of jellyfish, but it's the trailing tentacles you have to watch out for.

Because tentacles cannot sting through protective clothing, when diving in areas populated with coelenterates the best protection is a full wet suit, including gloves, booties, and hood. Stinging cells can attach to clothing, however, so if you come in contact with a jellyfish or one of its relatives, use extreme care in removing clinging tentacles.

Eels and Sea Snakes

The moray eel is a long, serpentlike fish that lives in holes in and around reefs, emerging only to forage for food. A moment of terror can be struck in a diver's heart the first time he peers into a small cave and sees a pair of beady eyes and a wicked set of jaws lined with needle-sharp teeth. Despite its fearsome appearance, the moray is not a dangerous creature except when frightened or molested. Some patient and fearless divers have even managed to feed morays from their hand.

Before reaching into any hole, even if you're certain it hides the biggest lobster or abalone in the world, check it visually to make sure it harbors nothing else. If you're foolish enough to spear a moray, you're in for a real battle because a wounded 6-foot eel becomes a powerful mass of raging muscle and snapping jaws that can slide right up the spear shaft to reach you.

A bite from a moray may range from a ragged wound to loss of a sizable chunk of flesh. In either unfortunate event, medical help is in order.

With divers exploring new areas around the world, the sea snake has gained prominence as a potentially dangerous creature. Some four dozen species of sea snakes inhabit waters of the South Pacific and the Indian Ocean, and

Beware the moray eel, who lurks and leers in rocky places. Looking much more evil than it really is, the moray usually withdraws at sight of a diver, becoming bold only when surprised or disturbed by an exploring hand. If you should have a finger seized by a moray, you can either try to pull loose and chance losing some flesh (you won't budge the eel), or calmly wait until it decides to let you go.

many of them are poisonous to man. Ranging in length from 3 to 9 feet, sea snakes are true reptiles but can remain underwater for a long time. They may be encountered on the bottom in shallows or swimming freely far from shore.

Most authorities agree that a ¼-inch wet suit gives protection from a bite. Nevertheless, if you see a snake in the water, give it a wide berth.

Victims of sea snake bites should be kept quiet, and antivenin treatment immediately is a must.

Octopus, Squid, and Barracuda

The blue-ringed octopus of Australia is a venomous creature that should be given a wide berth. Other than it, the octopus is one of diving's most exaggerated "monsters." Though possessing a powerful biting beak, it is timid and is usually seen hiding. Most species are relatively small, but in Washington's Puget Sound huge ones with a tentacle spread of 20 feet are common. The octopus likes snug, dark places, so watch where you reach.

Squid have a torpedo-shaped, streamlined body and are generally seen swimming in large schools. Like the octopus, squid have a parrotlike beak but, unless you grab one directly, a squid is of no danger.

The great barracuda is found mostly in warm Florida waters and throughout the Caribbean. It grows to lengths in excess of 6 feet, almost a fourth of that being a long, sleek head housing a mouth lined with several rows of sharp teeth. Though fearsome to behold, the barracuda has seldom been known to attack a diver, though one may streak like lightning for a diver's freshly speared fish.

The barracuda is curious and is thought to be attracted to shiny objects that reflect light underwater. Caribbean divers recommend putting a coat of black paint over chrome regulator parts or face mask rims in order not to tempt barracudas.

The alligator gar is a freshwater fish not unlike the barracuda in its sleekness and array of sharp teeth. A good-sized gar may weigh as much as two hundred pounds and be 6 or 7 feet long. Gar attacks on divers are rare, but they have happened. Another inhabitant of fresh water is the snapping turtle, which can inflict a nasty bite on a hand that gets too close for its comfort.

Stingrays, Venomous Fishes

An unwary wader who suddenly feels a sharp, stabbing pain in the leg can be pretty certain he's stepped on a stingray. Common in sandy bays, lagoons, and

The barracuda has an appearance more fearsome than his behavior. Divers have moved unmolested through large schools of curious barracudas, which apparently were more interested in what the swimmers were doing than in attacking them.

river mouths, stingrays (or stingarees) lie partially buried with only their eyes and a portion of their tails exposed. Their bodies are flat and round or diamond shaped, perfectly adapted to bottom dwelling. Most coastal rays average 20 inches in width, though some may be as much as 6 feet across. Even the smallest of these creatures possesses a whiplike tail armed with a saw-toothed spine that gives a ragged wound.

When wading in an area where stingrays are suspected or known to dwell, shuffle your feet as you walk over the bottom to give them fair warning. Usually rays will feel the underwater vibrations and get out of your way by flapping off and reburying themselves in the sand.

A laceration from a stingray burns like fire and may become infected. Rinse the area with fresh water to remove mucus left by the stinger and to help relieve the pain, soak in very hot water for thirty minutes, and seek medical attention as soon as possible.

Deep-water manta rays are related to stingrays. Although they may reach a grand width of more than 20 feet, they are harmless creatures. Some divers once considered it exciting to spear giant mantas, but since they are not food fish and cause no harm to anyone, they are now left pretty much alone.

A stingray's "stinger" is a saw-edged spine 2 to 6 inches long. When disturbed, the ray whips its tail up and over its back, and anything in the way, such as a wader's leg, may be severely lacerated by the spine.

Divers who are not fortunate enough to be able to dive often in tropical waters are unlikely to encounter venomous fishes. More than two hundred species of fish can deliver a venom by stinging or puncturing, and most are shallow-swimming or bottom-dwelling types, easily approachable by a skin diver. The poison is usually a toxic protein, secreted in pointed spines of the dorsal region. It is delivered involuntarily when the glandular tissue is ruptured by the mere touch of a diver's hand or foot.

The deadliest species of venomous fish are members of the scorpion fish group, which includes the scorpion fish proper, the stonefish, and the lionfish. Small, beautiful in color, and nonaggressive, venomous fish swim slowly or lie close to the bottom, looking deceptively harmless.

Symptoms of stings are not pleasant. They include intense pain, localized numbness, swelling, and, in severe cases, paralysis, convulsions, and possibly death. The most effective first-aid treatment is a hot-water bath of the wounded area and surrounding parts. With sufficient heat the poisonous protein is denatured and pain will subside quickly. Antivenin treatment is recommended.

The Unpredictable Shark

Perhaps the most dangerous of all marine creatures—and certainly the most enigmatic—is the shark. All manner of studies and experiments have been carried out to enable man to learn more about shark behavior and to predict the shark's reactions under certain conditions. What has been learned is that sharks are altogether unpredictable.

At one time researchers believed that such tricks as shouting underwater, blowing bubbles, banging on a scuba tank with a rock, or making frantic motions would frighten sharks. Over the years scientists have devised water-soluble dyes, flavors, essences, and repellents thought to be repulsive to sharks. Although humans have convinced themselves of the success of such devices, sharks have not. Some species of sharks are not frightened by the approach of a diver or anything he may do, including making faces, which was once thought to be a sure defense.

Only recently have researchers developed a repellent that the U.S. Navy claims to be 100 percent effective, and it is a form of common laundry detergent. As private companies refine a system for releasing the repellent, it will become widely used by the commercial, military, scientific, and sport diving communities.

As a diver you may never encounter a shark more fierce than a lethargic sand shark, dogfish, or leopard shark, all small species that do more harm to fishing nets than to swimmers. Nevertheless, you should be aware of species for which there are documented cases of attacks on humans. Also, you should know what to do if you meet up with a shark that stays around for more than a passing glance.

The following members of the shark family are large in size and have been known to attack swimmers or divers. Consequently, they should be considered extremely dangerous.

Great White. May be 30 feet or more in length and weigh several thousand pounds. Huge body with conical head and snout and pointed dorsal and pectoral fins. Has a gray back and white belly, but may be entirely leaden white. Large concentrations off Australia, but has been seen in most temperate seas and even in colder Northern California waters.

Great Hammerhead. As much as 15 feet in length. Flat head shaped like a tack hammer, with eyes and nostrils at the ends. Swings head from side to side when homing in on prey. Pointed fins and an asymmetrical tail with the upper lobe being the longer. Often swims with dorsal and tail fin out of water. Grayish color. Found around piers and reefs in temperate waters.

Blue sharks, often seen in large schools, are responsible for frequent swimmer attacks in Australia and on some coasts of Great Britain. The blue is fearless and quite aggressive.

Mako. Length to 12 feet. Long, pointed snout, rounded fins, pointed tail lobes. Bluish gray on back, white belly. One of the fastest-swimming sharks, inhabiting warm seas and shallow waters.

Tiger. Length to 20 feet or more. Large, broad head. Young tigers may have dark brown stripes on a grayish brown background; the barred patterns usually fade on adults. Habitats are Indian Ocean and tropical Pacific waters.

Blue. Length 10 to 12 feet. Long, pointed snout. Short, rounded dorsal fin; long, pointed pectoral fins. Upper body deep blue in color, underside white. Very aggressive. Feeds on surface fish. Found in warm seas and off the Southern California coast.

The best safeguard against shark trouble is avoidance. If you see a shark, get out of the area and out of the water. Sharks should never be annoyed or provoked, nor should you attempt to attack one. The following suggestions are applicable when diving in shark waters.

1. Never dive by yourself. Two sets of eyes are better than one set in spotting a shark and keeping it in view while retreating.

2. Do not dangle arms or legs from floats or boats and, when diving, keep below the surface as much as possible. Generally, sharks are more attracted to movement near the surface.

3. If you cut yourself, leave the water immediately, no matter how small the wound or how little it bleeds, so that sharks won't be attracted by the smell of blood.

4. When moving away from a shark, stay close to the bottom, near rocks, or next to a reef wall, swimming with regular, even strokes. Do not make any rapid motions, because panic moves attract sharks. Keep the shark in view at all times.

5. Do not dive in murky, dirty water. A shark may attack because to it you look like a large fish.

6. If spear fishing, do not tow your catch or fasten it to your belt. Get it out of the water. Never attach it to your body, even on a long stringer. Blood and wounded fish attract sharks like magnets.

7. Trying to spear a shark or attack it with a knife is foolhardy. A shark billy 2 to 3 feet long can be effective in fending off an attacker, especially if the end is studded with nails to keep it from slipping off the shark's skin.

In Case of an Accident

Rescue and First Aid

Even in the company of experienced, well-trained divers, accidents can occur because the underwater world is an unpredictable place and humans are not yet fully at home there. Because a doctor isn't always likely to be present at a dive site, every diver should be capable of handling incidents quickly and knowledgeably. If you know what to do when someone is in distress or injured, and act promptly, you may be the means of preserving that person's life.

A course in lifesaving would be beneficial but is not essential if you can grasp and perform the rescue techniques described in the following pages. Most are adapted from procedures developed by the National Association of Underwater Instructors and other instructional organizations. Through actual use they have proved their worth many times over. The basic procedures are taken from Red Cross practices, and a knowledge of them could help prevent a mishap from becoming a casualty, but they are only a minimum. A thorough course of training is valuable beyond measure.

181

ASSISTING A TIRED DIVER

Many diving accidents need never have developed if the victim had been assisted by his buddy or a nearby diver. Every diver should be capable of recognizing signs of distress and must not wait for the person in trouble to ask for help. When someone begins thrashing about and rejects his snorkel or scuba mouthpiece, he is probably exhausted beyond the point of thinking in a rational way and needs assistance.

When you notice such behavior at the surface, calmly ask the diver to inflate his flotation vest and/or drop his weight belt. This will make him more buoyant and get his head out of the water. If he cannot release his belt, you may have to submerge in front of him and unbuckle it, letting it fall free. Once he is loosed of his weights, ask him to lie back and remove his face mask, then inhale and exhale easily through his nose and mouth. In his anxiety he may be breathing hard, so caution against hyperventilating.

If a surf mat or paddleboard is available, push it to the diver. You can also swim around behind and support him under the arm with one hand while using your other hand to help inflate his vest. If he forces you to kick hard to remain on the surface, you may have to inflate your own vest.

Once the diver has calmed a little, you can grasp his ankles and push him ahead of you toward shore. Or you can hold his tank valve and pull him behind as you swim along using a sidestroke. As rescuer, be on guard against fatiguing yourself or towing the other diver into a situation that you cannot cope with.

Although an assisting hand is sometimes actually needed, the mere presence of a calm buddy will often be enough to help a tired diver regain composure and self-confidence.

RESCUING A DIVER IN SERIOUS TROUBLE

On occasion a diver will be so thoroughly exhausted or so overcome by panic that he will be incapable of helping himself. In going to the rescue of a seriously distressed person, try to utilize some form of flotation equipment to help the victim and to keep yourself safe.

Surface Rescue Using a Flotation Device

When a distressed diver is conscious, push a surf mat ahead of you, drifting it straight toward him so he can grab it and support himself. While he's resting you can comfort him by holding his hands or arms across the mat. If an unconscious victim is wearing a tank, ditch it before commencing rescue with a flotation device. An unconscious victim will generally float face down with both arms extended. Lying lengthwise on a mat as you approach, paddle over the diver from behind. When the front of the mat is over his head, reach down on both sides and give him a big bear hug, then roll all the way to left or right, turning the mat completely over. As long as you hold on tightly as you roll, the victim will end up lying on his back on top of the mat.

If you, the rescuer, are much smaller than the victim, lie crosswise on the mat as you approach. Swim the front edge of the mat up against the back of the victim's neck, then reach over one of his shoulders and across his chest, holding him securely. With your other hand push down on the back edge of the mat and arch yourself backward. The mat will invert, bringing the victim up onto it on his back. Whenever you have someone on a surf mat, be sure he is centered or else the mat will slip out from under.

Although inner tubes are not the best of surface floats, they can be effective in rescue situations. If the tube has a game bag attached to its center, use it like a surf mat, rolling the victim over onto it. If the center is open, get the victim's arms over the top of the tube and through the center, then flip the tube over his head and force it down under his armpits. Spread his arms to help keep him from falling out of the tube.

When using a paddleboard or a surfboard, sit astride it and get hold of the victim's wrists. Pull him over the board, grabbing the bottom of his tank or the seat of his protective suit.

Even if the beach is the closest point of safety, do not take a victim on a board through heavy surf because a hurtling, solid float can incapacitate both victim and rescuer. Instead, stay behind the breaker line and call for help, or else abandon the board and use the cross-chest carry to negotiate the rough, inshore water.

Surface Rescue Without a Flotation Device

A conscious person in need of rescue at the surface may be quite passive. On the other hand, a violent victim should be approached quickly and with great caution. Close in from behind if possible, or else make a surface dive well in front of him. Underwater, grasp the victim by the knees and turn him around, then surface in back of him and reach over one shoulder to cup your hand around his chin. If surface conditions are calm, remove his face mask with your free hand; otherwise, leave it on. Regardless of the state of the water, remove his mask if you think he needs more air. Keeping his chin cupped, drop his weight belt and inflate his vest.

Once the victim is buoyant, pause a minute to catch your breath and take whatever steps are necessary to make yourself buoyant. Signal for help by holding one arm high and waving or by blowing a whistle, then start towing the diver toward safety by grasping his tank valve or the neck of his buoyancy compensator vest.

Resuscitation in the Water

When a diver is unconscious and floating on the surface, quick action and decisiveness are very important. Hesitating only a couple of minutes could prove fatal. Level off the victim by dropping his weight belt and inflating his vest. Ditch his tank only if it is in the way. Remove his face mask as well as your own, inflate your vest, and, if the victim is not breathing, commence mouth-to-mouth resuscitation (see details later in this chapter). Also check the victim's carotid artery, which lies behind the windpipe, for a pulse. If none is present, get him to the beach or a boat fast.

Mouth-to-mouth in the water is not easy, but it is possible if the rescuer keeps his wits about him. Turn the victim face up and tilt his head back far enough to open the air passage. You may have to lift up on the back of his neck to get his mouth open. If another diver is present, he can tow the victim while you administer mouth-to-mouth. If you haven't already removed his tank, get rid of it before reaching the beach.

On the beach or on a boat, lay the victim so his head is lower than his feet (scooping a hole under the head helps lower it and ensures a straight air passage). If there is no pulse, begin cardiopulmonary resuscitation immediately (details later). If pulse is present, administer mouth-to-mouth only.

Rescue of a Submerged Victim

Rescuing a submerged victim also requires quick action, so don't waste time checking him over. Regardless of condition, the victim must be brought to the surface. Approach the disabled diver from behind, tilting his head back with the chin carry to open his air passage. With your other arm, hug him by pushing your chest against his tank and your hand against the lower part of his rib cage. Kick off for the surface and, as you rise, squeeze him hard to force expanding air out of his lungs, thus preventing an embolism. Don't drop the victim's weight belt or inflate his vest until you hit the surface. While ascending, be sure to ventilate your own lungs, since you will more than likely be going up faster than you should.

On reaching the surface, signal for help, then drop the victim's weight belt, inflate his vest, and start mouth-to-mouth resuscitation if he is not breathing. A victim who recovers on the surface may throw up, go into shock, or start to panic, so be prepared for any reaction.

Rescue in Surf

One of the most dangerous situations for Samaritan as well as sufferer is a beach rescue. Whenever you are on shore and spot someone beginning a surf exit, keep an eye on him and be prepared to help. If you go to the aid of a diver who is in obvious need of assistance in surf, don't get dumped yourself. Standing in the shallows, reach around his body and drop his weight belt, grab his tank valve, and tell him to crawl out of the water. Don't lift up on the tank and don't try to help the diver to his feet, since hoisting at his armpits prevents him from moving under his own steam. He may be numb from cold and worn out from the wave action, and if so you'll have to literally drag him up onto the beach. You'll be able to handle yourself and aid someone else better on the beach if you drop your tank and fins before rushing to help.

Divers have drowned just behind the surf line because a rescuer did not get out there fast enough. If you are wearing a wet suit and go after someone, you'll need fins and a weight belt, too, in case you have to dive for him; if he remains on the surface, you can ditch your belt when you reach him. Handle the situation as you would a surface rescue of a conscious victim. Stay well behind the surf until the victim has regained breath and composure, then assist him in on the surface. Signaling to the beach will alert other divers to stand by.

TREATMENT FOR HYPOTHERMIA

Loss of body heat due to difference in specific heat of air and water is a phenomenon familiar to all divers. Even when wearing a protective suit, shivering during and after a dive is usually accepted as part of the sport. But if the body becomes chilled beyond a certain point, the dangerous malady known as hypothermia may result.

Hypothermia is an excessive loss of body heat. Its early symptoms include uncontrollable shivering, muscle rigidity, and numbness, followed by mental confusion, slowness in movement, and slowness of breathing. If relief is not forthcoming, unconsciousness and death may follow.

Since hypothermia is loss of body heat, the treatment is immediate active rewarming. The quickest way of reheating is to get the victim out of the open air and into a hot bath. Next best is dry clothing, blankets, or a sleeping bag. Huddling bodies are an excellent source of external heat, and internal heat can be provided by hot liquids.

Hypothermia can be avoided by getting plenty of rest before diving, eating high-carbohydrate meals, wearing an adequate protective suit, and not making deep dives.

MOUTH-TO-MOUTH RESUSCITATION

When respiration has stopped, rescue breathing must be started immediately. Seconds are valuable because, after four minutes of nonbreathing, oxygen starvation has begun brain damage. Though distasteful to squeamish individuals, mouth-to-mouth has proven the most simple and effective method of encouraging resumption of the respiratory cycle. Don't delay; the first inflations are the most important.

1. Lay the victim on his back and tilt his head back so his chin points up. This opens the air passage and moves the tongue away from the back of the throat.

2. From a position at the side of the victim's head, open your mouth and place it firmly over his open mouth. Pinch his nostrils shut with one hand.

3. Blow into the victim's mouth with three quick breaths. If his air passage is open, his chest will expand.

4. Remove your mouth and allow the air to escape from his lungs.

5. Repeat the cycle, at the rate of about twelve breaths a minute for an adult, more for a child.

If you feel resistance to your blowing, the victim's airway may be blocked. Turn him on his side and apply three or four sharp blows between his shoulder blades with the palm of your hand. If foreign matter is visible at his mouth, clear it away before resuming mouth-to-mouth.

CARDIOPULMONARY RESUSCITATION

If after nine or ten inflations by mouth-to-mouth the victim is not breathing or has not regained normal color, or if there is no carotid pulse, you should artificially compress his heart to force oxygenated blood to the brain and other vital organs. The following steps are essential in administering CPR.

     1. Begin with mouth-to-mouth resuscitation to ventilate the victim's lungs.

     2. Place one hand flat over the lower part of his breastbone and place the other hand on top of it.

     3. Press straight down firmly toward the spine, then release.

     4. After fifteen compressions, at the rate of eighty per minute, stop and inflate the victim's lungs twice within five seconds by mouth-to-mouth. (If two rescuers are available, compress the heart at the rate of once per second, then inflate the lungs once after five compressions.)

     5. Continue compressions and inflations until recovery or arrival of medical help.

     Caution: Do not try to improve your cardiopulmonary resuscitation technique by practicing on a living person. Mannequins are used for this purpose. If you desire a formal training program in CPR, contact your local Heart Association or discuss the matter with a diving instructor.

FOLLOW UP WITH FIRST AID

Getting a diver out of a hazardous situation quickly is usually only the first measure in saving him. An accident victim may be physically injured and will often be in a state of shock. Both conditions require immediate attention. First aid is emergency help, a stopgap until medical care is available. If you are called upon to administer to a victim, three basic steps should be taken immediately:

     1. Check for breathing. When breathing is suspended for even a short period, brain damage and death may result. If the victim is not breathing, don't delay in starting mouth-to-mouth resuscitation. If there is no response, check for a pulse and be prepared to commence cardiopulmonary resuscitation.

     2. Check for bleeding. Depending on the location and nature of a wound, rapid loss of blood can cause unconsciousness and death, so stop

bleeding as rapidly as possible. Apply direct pressure to stem the flow, but be careful not to press so hard that you stop circulation. If bleeding continues, seek out arterial pressure points (see the following section).

3. Check for shock. Nearly all accident victims will suffer some form of shock. Shock has been known to cause death even though an injury was not serious. The first signs are loss of facial color; cold, moist skin; and a rapid but weak pulse. Shallow, irregular breathing and fainting are common. To offset shock, keep the victim warm and elevate his feet. If he is conscious, try to calm him. Loosen his clothing, especially around the head and neck.

Treatment of Bleeding

With certain types of wounds, some bleeding is desirable because it helps cleanse the area of foreign matter. However, severe bleeding can be fatal if it continues unchecked. Cover a wound that flows freely with a clean cloth and apply hand pressure directly over the dressing. If this doesn't help, pressure must be applied to arteries supplying blood to the wounded area.

To control heavy bleeding in an arm or a hand, press with your fingers against the inside of the upper arm, halfway between the elbow and the armpit. If bleeding is from a leg or a foot, press with the heel of your hand against the victim's pelvic bone midway along the crease between the body and the thigh, on the same side of the body as the wound. Do not use a tourniquet unless you are unable to control bleeding any other way.

Once the flow of blood has been checked, flood the area with clean, fresh water, if available, and elevate the injury higher than the heart to inhibit further bleeding. Apply a sterile compress and bandage, but don't bind too tightly. For a puncture, remove whatever object made the wound, using tweezers if necessary (as you might have to do in getting out a sea urchin spine). Encourage bleeding by pressing gently on the sides of the injured area. Apply a sterile dressing. If the wound is deep or pain persists, get the patient to a doctor.

Treatment of Broken Bones

Surge may throw a diver against a rock or a coral head with enough violence to fracture an arm or a leg. Suspect a broken bone if there is a deformity in a limb, accompanied by local swelling, pain, and difficulty of movement.

Do not move a person with a broken bone unless it's necessary to get him into a safe locale. Place the injured limb in as normal a position as possible, apply an emergency splint to support the point of break, and immobilize the

---

DIVER'S FIRST-AID KIT

A first-aid kit should be considered an essential part of your diving gear and should not be far from hand during every dive. The following items are basic; local conditions or personal taste may suggest additional articles.

50 all-purpose adhesive bandages (such as Band-Aid)
1 gauze bandage, 1 inch wide
1 gauze bandage, 2 inches wide
Adhesive tape, 1 inch wide
6 gauze pads, various sizes
Cotton swabs
Medicated stick (such as Chap Stick)
Sunburn screen lotion (such as PABA)
Motion sickness tablets (such as Bonine or Dramamine)
Decongestant tablets (such as Sudafed)
Isopropyl alcohol (about 70 percent solution, for cleansing the external
  ear canal)
Germicide spray (such as Bactine)
Antibiotic ointment (such as Neosporin)
Bar of soap
Scissors
Tweezers
Needle

---

limb until medical help can be obtained. A splint can be improvised from almost anything rigid: a couple of straight sticks, a length of board, an oar, even a spear gun. Fasten it to the injured limb by tying it snugly in at least three places with strips of cloth, but do not tie it so tight that circulation is cut off.

Heart Failure

Heart failure, or cardiac arrest, can easily be mistaken for other maladies because many of the symptoms are similar. The face of a person suffering a heart attack will sometimes be flushed, or may be very pale; the victim may have bluish lips and fingernails. He may show signs of difficulty in breathing. Often there is agonizing chest pain.

If the victim is conscious, keep him absolutely quiet and lying down unless he's more comfortable in a semisitting position. Make sure that he is warm and stay close to provide moral support, summoning medical help immediately. Do not offer a heart attack victim anything to drink. If the victim is unconscious and heart failure is suspected, follow the steps given earlier under Cardiopulmonary Resuscitation. Begin with mouth-to-mouth resuscitation and follow immediately with closed-heart massage.

Cardiopulmonary resuscitation can mean the difference between life and death. Every diver should be familiar with the techniques.

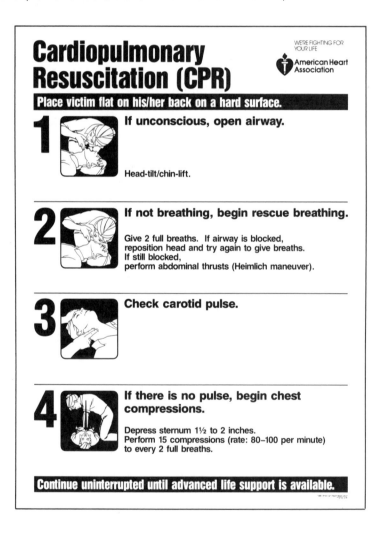

10

Now That You're a Diver

Putting Your Scuba Skills to Use

Once certified, some divers are content to return to the water only once or twice a year. Many others spend long weekends, vacations, and odd holidays seeking out new sites or exploring the same ones over and over again. A few put their training and experience to practical use and embark on lifetime careers in underwater work. There is no limit to the ways an eager diver can use diving skills.

Schools, dive shops, and recreation departments are certifying hundreds of new divers every few months. Expanding interest and increasing numbers of enthusiasts have put so many people into the water that local sites have often become crowded. Divers are traveling to exotic shores in faraway places. Around the world, especially in the Caribbean and the South Pacific, resort hotels are catering more and more to the traveling diver. Many places have complete equipment rental facilities, provide modern boats to speed guests to the diving areas, and furnish guides or native divers to take them to the best sites.

Certain travel agencies cater to divers, handling all the details for transportation, lodging, and diving. A good agent can save you time and trouble, give you ideas for planning an itiner-

191

ary, and suggest places you never knew existed. One of the best sources for listings of diver travel agencies, as well as for well-written articles on diving, is *Skin Diver,* a magazine available on newsstands or through subscription.

TO SPEAR OR NOT TO SPEAR

One of the hottest controversies in the history of diving was sparked late in 1973 by the appearance in *Skin Diver* of an article by Philippe Cousteau, son of the inventor of the Aqua-Lung. The story was brief but straight to the point, and the point was that spearfishing simply for the sake of killing is not a sport but a serious threat to the marine environment. For months the magazine was swamped with letters pro and con on the subject, each offering its own forcible reasoning, each attacking the other's arguments. Nothing was ever resolved, of course, but the tremendous response from divers everywhere made it clear that spearfishing is a very touchy subject among those who find their pleasure underwater.

Many novice divers, having read of the ocean's teeming fish populations, enter the sea expecting the sun to be darkened by vast schools of swimming life. But fish are not as plentiful as they once were because commercial fisheries, pollution, and other killers of fish have taken a considerable toll. How about divers? Well, the California Department of Fish and Game made an extensive study of fish populations in areas frequented by spearfishermen during the period 1958 to 1972, and their conclusions were that divers brought in less than 1 percent (0.67 percent) of total fish by numbers.

If you choose to spearfish, you can go about it in either of two ways: you can free dive (skin dive) or you can hunt as a scuba diver. If you decide that free diving is more to your liking, you should be in excellent physical condition, able to dive deep, and capable of staying down for a long time. Hunting only on the amount of air you can hold in a breath, you are at a disadvantage compared with the fish you seek, and to some divers this is more of a true sport. However, a good free diver is sometimes able to spear more fish than a scuba diver can because he does not emit noisy bubbles, which send much sea life scurrying away. A scuba diver, on the other hand, has the time to inspect game more carefully and stalk it with more leisure, firing only when certain of making a quick kill.

Novice spearfishermen often tend to spear undersized game and even nonedible species. In the interest of sportsmanship, it's a good idea to learn to recognize edible fish and to leave the others alone.

The following suggestions are offered for diver safety as well as out of consideration for the natural underwater life.

1. Treat all spear guns like high-powered rifles.
2. Do not load a spear gun on a boat or a beach.
3. Keep a gun on safety until you're ready to fire it.
4. When spearfishing, stay a safe distance from other divers.
5. Know what you're aiming at and make sure it isn't a person.
6. Spear only what you intend to eat, never killing wantonly.
7. Unload a gun before leaving the water and remove the spearhead from the shaft.
8. Put a cork or a rubber protector over the spearhead.

If you learn to be a proficient spearfisherman, you may want to become competitive about your prowess. The United States holds national contests in spearfishing, and winners may compete in world championships. Because meets are well-organized, there is never wholesale slaughter, and disposition of all fish to needy groups is arranged beforehand. Team members must meet their own expenses. Thus this kind of spearfishing remains as one of the few real athletic competitions and one of the toughest that can be truly classified as an amateur sport.

HUNTING WITH A CAMERA

A way of enjoying the thrills of a hunt without spearing or trapping is to capture the prey for all time on film. Underwater photography as a pastime is now surpassing spearfishing, as is evidenced by the increasingly wide selection of photographic equipment in dive shops.

Watertight housings are made for many models of dry-land cameras, so if you are even halfway skillful at taking pictures, bring your camera to a good dive shop to find out if it can be "containerized." If you're handy with tools, you might consider fabricating your own Plexiglas housing, bringing the extensions for focusing, winding, and shutter release outside the case. Remember that a housing must be absolutely watertight, since even a few drops of salt water can ruin both film and camera.

To test a housing without risking the camera, attach a few pounds of weight to it and lower it on a line to a depth of about 5 feet, watching for telltale air bubbles. If you don't see any, lower the unit to 20 or 30 feet, then retrieve it. If the inside is dry, the housing will probably be safe for a camera.

The Nikonos submersible camera is one of the most widely used pieces of photographic equipment available. It is compact, lightweight, easy to operate, reliable, takes excellent pictures, and is moderately priced. Little wonder that it is favored by amateurs and used extensively by professionals. The Nikonos uses no bulky housing. You simply load a standard roll of 35-millimeter film into it on dry land, then take the camera right into the water. You can shoot pictures above the surface as well as below, using a wide variety of interchangeable lenses. The Nikonos V features automatic exposure.

For accurate exposures, especially when using the more critical color films, you should use an underwater light meter. If you already own a meter, you may be able to build a watertight housing for it from Plexiglas. Otherwise, try to find a case that fits it, or else buy an amphibious light meter.

Near the surface there is usually enough available natural light for picture taking, but even a few feet down you'll find that a supplementary light source is necessary for bright, snappy shots. You can use underwater flash or electronic strobe lights. The strobe lights require no bulb changing. Before deciding either way, talk with other diving photographers to obtain a cross section of opinion and preference. If you decide on flash, remember that litter in the sea is just as bad as litter on the land; don't discard used bulbs on the spot, but take them ashore with you and get rid of them in a proper place.

DIVING AT NIGHT

Diving after the sun has set is becoming increasingly popular with divers who have a little experience behind them and want to get acquainted with another of the many moods of the underwater realm. Many marine creatures are nocturnal, showing themselves to the inquisitive eye only after dark. At night the daytime swimmers rest motionlessly among rocks, kelp stalks, and coral branches, seemingly fast asleep, and they often allow a diver to approach closely and even touch them before darting away. There is an aura of mystery and adventure in night diving that appeals to many.

The diving skills required for nighttime excursions are like those needed during the day, only sharper. Greater attention must be paid to suiting up, to entering and exiting, to underwater movements. And even greater regard for buddy cooperation is essential.

You should dive only in areas with which you are thoroughly familiar, visiting the site the morning of the same day to get an idea of bottom conditions and obstructions. Diving from a boat is the safest way to enter the water, but if a boat isn't available, don't curtail your pleasure by not diving. As long as the surf is very small and the area isn't rocky, you can enter and exit from a beach. If strong currents are running, do not dive. Also avoid night diving in heavy kelp or turbid water.

Check out your equipment during daylight hours and dress either in a lighted place or on the beach just before sunset. Each diver should have his own underwater light (with fresh batteries and a wrist loop), a luminous depth gauge, a compass, and a whistle attached by a short length of line to his vest. The whistle is a good means of locating your buddy on the surface or of getting attention on a boat or ashore. If the diving area is relatively free of marine entanglements, buddies can hold the ends of an 8- to 10-foot safety line.

When diving from a boat, hang a high-intensity light beneath the keel as a homing beacon and dive within sight of it. If diving from the beach, set a lantern or other light source 3 or 4 feet above ground so you can spot it when surfacing offshore.

Underwater visibility is limited by the power of your light beam, so minimize your activity and slow down your swimming speed. Unless you and your buddy work out an involved code of tugs on a safety line or squeezes on an arm, hand signals are especially important at night. To communicate, first get your buddy's attention by flashing your light on and off, or reach over and gently tap him on the shoulder. Grabbing him suddenly may startle the day-lights out of him, and shining your light directly in his eyes will ensure his not being able to enjoy the rest of the dive.

In pitch-black water it's easy to become disoriented and lose all sense of up or down. By using your light, you can watch to see which way bubbles go and follow them to the surface. In the unlikely event that your light—as well as your buddy's light—fails, keep an eye on your luminous depth gauge and head for the smaller number readings.

EXPLORING SUBMARINE CAVES

Some adventurous sport divers who have dived time and time again to poke around coral reefs or push through kelp beds turn to underwater caves for new worlds of exploration. In many inland regions of the world, far from the sea, caves, sinkholes, and springs afford the only diving. Cave diving brings into play all normal scuba skills plus some highly specialized techniques that have been developed for this very challenging environment.

Being a skilled open-water diver isn't enough of a qualification for coping with the potential hazards of cave diving. A diver cannot expect to continue exploring an underwater cave until his air supply is low and then switch on his reserve valve to make an exit; usually, as much air is needed to get *out* of a cave as was used to penetrate it. In a cave a diver can't rely on a free ascent in an emergency because there is usually no direct route to the surface. Cave divers must know how to use a guideline to find their way back to the entrance. They must be prepared for total darkness, silting (murky water), and disorientation, a few of the several hazards that in all likelihood will be unfamiliar to an open-water diver.

Divers entering a cave must mentally adjust to being in a confined environment and to the ever-present danger of becoming lost. They must totally discount the idea of being able to reach the surface quickly whenever they want. And they must rely heavily on mechanical equipment, such as lights, guidelines, buoyancy compensators, and auxiliary breathing devices.

Lights should be rugged, equipped with fresh batteries, and capable of giving full-power illumination for the duration of the dive. A diving light should be used only for diving, not as a camp flashlight. Most experienced cave divers use a main light as well as a safety backup unit.

Using a safety reel and line is the only sure way back to the surface. A reel should be compact, should operate smoothly, and should hold as much as 500 feet of braided nylon line.

Maintaining neutral buoyancy is especially important in cave diving because of the limited amount of space for maneuvering one's body. Proper buoyancy is also necessary to avoid stirring up silt. To obtain neutral buoyancy, cave divers use a variety of equipment: constant-volume tanks, plastic bottles, cans, and buoyancy compensator vests. Experienced cave divers should be consulted by anyone planning a cave dive in a new place, since different sites may require different equipment arrangements.

Provision for an emergency air supply or a means of sharing air is mandatory. Some divers prefer an auxiliary buddy tank of 20- to 40-cubic-feet size, or a small pony bottle holding 12 cubic feet of air, with its own regulator. Other divers prefer an octopus rig—one first stage with two second stages. Just remember that with two divers using one tank, the air goes at least twice as fast.

Cave diving requires tight advance planning for every dive. Some experts in this very specialized sport recommend allocation of air supply as one third in, one third out, and one third for a safety margin. In addition, they suggest the following rules:

1. Never dive alone.

2. Use a sturdy guideline tied at the cave's mouth.

3. Stay within arm's reach of your guideline.

4. Avoid passageways where you cannot turn around easily.

5. Beware of crumbling walls and ceilings and guard against stirring up silt.

DIVING UNDER ICE

If you've ever been hardy enough to don scuba gear and ease yourself through a yawning hole chopped in the frozen surface of a quarry or a lake, you're one of a zealous species of underwater fanatics known as ice divers. An out-of-the-ordinary branch of sport diving, ice diving requires one to be physically fit, a bit daring without being foolhardy, and maybe just a little daft.

Why do some divers stand around in subzero temperatures and submerge themselves in bone-numbing waters? Many do it because it brings a sense of achievement, of carrying out something few others would dare, or care, to attempt. Others ice dive because of the sparkling clarity of inland waters during winter months.

You should select a dive site that you are familiar with from previous summer dives. You should have a fair knowledge of the area's depths, its marine life, and its potential snares. Before a dive, check all equipment very carefully. Because regulators have been known to freeze up or fail, an octopus rig is advisable. Some divers favor a two-hose regulator for ice diving because the large diaphragm gives some protection to the high-pressure orifices, making them less susceptible to freezing. A hint: Test breathe through your regulator *indoors* where the temperature is warm. If you do it outdoors just before entering the water, condensation from your breath will almost certainly freeze in the regulator before you can use it below the surface.

For short dives a ¼- or ¾-inch Farmer John-style wet suit will suffice. Three-finger mittens will keep hands warmer than gloves, and a pair of wool socks worn under booties will be more comfortable than booties alone. For longer dives, a dry suit worn over a sweat shirt and sweat pants, or over a complete wet suit, will do a good job of retaining body heat. Keep warm while suiting up. A windbreak will decrease chilling from wind while preparing for the dive, and a small nearby shelter with a propane heating unit can be very cozy.

Locate the entry/exit hole in such a place that snowmobiles will not roar into it. Cut a squarish block out of the ice at least 4 feet on a side, large enough to accommodate two or three divers. Cutting with a chain saw is less fatiguing than with the muscle-powered variety. Force the block down under the surface of the surrounding ice. (After a dive, be sure to replace the block so no one will fall into the hole.)

Making an ice dive involves much more than swimming around awhile and then emerging. Contrary to popular belief, underneath the ice there are no trapped pockets of air that you can breathe in case of emergency. If you run low on air or have problems, there is only one way out of the water and that is through the hole you entered.

To assure finding the hole again, ice divers use a safety line. This is a 200-foot length of nylon or polypropylene rope ¼ inch or more in diameter, with one end tied to a tree. The other end is tied around the waist of the lead diver; then each diver of two-man buddy teams links himself to it by tying one end of a 10-foot length of rope securely around his upper arm and attaching the other end to the safety line by a well-knotted loop that is free to slide up and down. One person, dressed for diving, is designated line tender, and his job is to remain at the edge of the hole, ready to enter the water or to haul in safety line and divers if the necessity arises.

A set of rope signals should be agreed upon in advance as a means by which divers can communicate with the line tender. Usually one yank signals "Trouble, haul in"; two means "Snag, hold steady"; three signifies "Take up slack." Rope signals are not standardized, so when diving with a group for the first time make sure everyone agrees on the signals.

When all is ready, the lead diver enters the water, swims out to the limit of the safety line, and commences swimming in a large circle whose center is the hole. Each diver enters and is free to swim the length of the line and 10 feet on either side of it. Even during the limited time you can stay down in 34° F. water (a 72-cubic-foot tank lasts twenty to thirty minutes), a surprising amount of area can be covered.

The safety line assures you of finding your way back and is a quick means of retrieval in case of trouble. Your life depends on the ropes, so before every dive inspect all knots and splices carefully.

If for some reason you lose the safety line as well as your buddy, do not swim about aimlessly. A natural but dangerous first reaction is to try frantically to find the other divers or get back to the hole. Instead, stay in the area but go *deeper*. When near the bottom, look up to spot the hole, since you're more likely to see it from a deeper vantage point than from a shallow oblique angle. When other divers realize that someone is off the line, they should immediately begin swimming in 20-foot-diameter circles, making visual sweeps downward.

Ice diving has its own set of thrills and pleasures. Instead of always swimming face down, turn over on your back to watch your exhaust bubbles shimmer as they rise and spread out when they hit the frozen surface. Or turn upside down and walk along on the underside of the surface ice. When in the water, swim slowly and deliberately, since sudden moves may cause a gap in your wet suit that will admit cold water.

Even though you are secured to a safety line, keep an eye on where you're swimming. Any body of water seems to invite dumping of junk, and it's not uncommon even in a small lake to encounter automobile bodies, mysterious pieces of discarded machinery, and rolls of rusted barbed wire. The latter is such a hazard in many parts of the country that local divers carry wire cutters in addition to their knives.

When emerging from the water after a dive, don't stand around on the ice in your wet suit because the water in it will probably freeze the minute you hit the air. To avoid chilling, get close to a fire or move indoors where it's warm. Take off your diving gear, change into dry clothing, and drink some warm soup.

THERE'S GOLD IN THOSE RIVERS

Since the mid-1950s a new kind of gold rush has spread over many parts of the country. Though not involving the masses of humanity that flowed into California a hundred years earlier, it is nevertheless a gold rush. And though the rewards may not be as great as those that occasionally fell to the lucky forty-niners who struck it rich, the modern miner usually works a lot less hard, has more fun doing it, and may easily earn enough in a week or a weekend to pay for his trip into the gold country.

The gear required by the gold diver is much the same as that worn by any other sport diver except that air tanks are replaced by a hookah rig (a demand regulator connected by hose to a compressor at the surface). In addition, a gold diver may have to wear as much as 50 pounds of weight to help him hold his own in fast-moving streams. A full protective suit is usually necessary because some streams are fed by melting snow or icy cold springs.

To gather the hoped-for riches, the diving argonaut uses a kind of submersible vacuum cleaner called an underwater dredge, a device consisting of a large-diameter metal pipe into which a gasoline-powered pump forces a strong jet of water. When the pipe is submerged, a suction is created that slurps up gravel, rocks, and anything else that will pass through its opening. The water and debris are passed over a riffle—a pan containing a grating or a series of baffles that trap heavier particles, such as gold.

To know where to look for gold, you should know how it got there. Over many thousands of years, streams and rivers have washed over gold-bearing rocks, carrying particles of the precious metal downstream. Gold, being heavier than the accompanying gravel and sand, tends to settle to the bottom of a streambed, becoming trapped in cracks and crevices there and along the downstream side of sharp bends in the water course. By seeking out such likely spots and applying the business end of a dredge to the bottom, sometimes helping matters by digging and scraping with a metal basting spoon, a patient diver may come away richer than when he started.

Good information on prospecting is available through the Division of Mines in your state or in Washington, D.C. Fields for prospecting are wide, because gold has been found in California, Nevada, Colorado, Idaho, Montana, South Dakota, North Carolina, Georgia, and Alaska. In most states you will need to obtain a dredging permit, usually from the State Department of Fish and Game, where you will be able to find out about areas open for prospecting. Even then, before beginning any operation, make sure you aren't trespassing on private property. Crude gold can be legally sold to commercial smelting and refining companies and to authorized dealers. For further information on federal laws concerning gold, write to the Office of Domestic Gold and Silver Operations, Washington, D.C. 20220.

Some gold divers build their own dredge from odd parts, pipes, and pumps. Others buy ready-made units from manufacturers listed in the telephone directory under "Dredging Equipment." You may be able to obtain information on equipment from local dive shops, hardware stores, or feed and fuel supply centers.

WRECK AND TREASURE DIVING

William Phips, the colonial American who recovered a fabulous treasure trove off Haiti in 1687, was not the first successful salvage diver, nor was he the last.

In 1960 Kip Wagner of Florida discovered the scattered remains of a 1715 Spanish fleet of ten or more ships that had been smashed to bits during a violent hurricane. Kip salvaged over four million dollars' worth of treasure —a mere fraction of the fleet's value. In the 1950s Harry Rieseberg, author of several books on sunken treasure, recovered nearly five million dollars' worth of bullion and artifacts from sunken ships in the Caribbean. And in 1973 Mel

Fisher, a former California dive-shop owner turned treasure hunter, discovered in the Florida Keys two Spanish galleons that had sunk in a 1622 hurricane. Their cargoes together were valued at more than one and a half million ducats, well over $200 million in today's currency.

Whether you desire to dive for coins, anchors, cannons, antique bottles, or other artifacts, once you start treasure hunting you will find yourself consumed by a fever that burns unlike anything else. Treasure diving can be great fun, but if you really get involved it can be an expensive enterprise. Every diver dreams of swimming onto a sunken ship lying intact in shallow, crystal-clear water. Reality seldom follows dreams, however, since most wooden ships have been attacked by worms or are covered with coral. Accidentally stumbling onto a wreck is a rare fluke. Usually you have to search them out in a planned, purposeful way, doing a great deal of research in advance and then making use of metal detectors and other sophisticated instruments.

If you want to dive for treasure along the United States coast, you should check with the government of the state you're interested in regarding salvage leases. You should also find out what claim that state has on findings. If insurance companies have claims on sunken ships, you will have to share your discovery with them. Most will allow you to deduct your expenses and retain about 20 percent of the total value.

If you get wind of a possible wreck, you will need to pinpoint its location, check back on the cargo it was carrying, and learn whether previous salvage attempts have been made. If you learn that everyone and his brother has already pawed over a sunken ship, you'll at least be mentally prepared for not finding anything left but the hull.

The archives of local newspapers are a good place to begin a hunt for records relating to sunken ships. You might also check with harbor masters, who may have old lighthouse keeper's logs. Public and university libraries may have books on sunken ships or marine tragedies. The U.S. Coast Guard in Washington, D.C., has for many decades maintained outstanding records on coastal mishaps and accidents. The Smithsonian Institution in Washington, D.C., is helpful in identifying objects and artifacts. When Kip Wagner was researching one of his early finds, he made a major discovery at the U.S. Library of Congress.

If you plan to research the Manila galleons that crisscrossed the seas during the fifteenth through the seventeenth centuries, you'll have to spend long hours in the Archives of the Indies in Seville, Spain. Most of the writings are in archaic Spanish, so you'll need to either know the language or enlist the help of someone who does. A little closer to home are the innumerable ships that have gone down in the Great Lakes or have sunk off the New England or California coasts. County or local historical societies often keep records of coastal events, and maritime museums are a good bet for research sources.

Even after you positively locate a wreck, diving may not be the snap you imagine it to be in your mind's eye. Weather and rough seas may keep you out of the water for weeks at a time; currents, extreme depths, and natural as well as manmade hazards may conspire to keep you from what may seem within your grasp. The *Andrea Doria* is a good example of a contemporary sunken ship that has already become a classic of sorts in the annals of wreck diving. Sunk in 1956 in the North Atlantic, the ship has been dived on many times but none of the forays could, by any exaggeration, be called easy. For most months of the year bad weather closes the area off entirely to salvage attempts. Working dives are between 150 and 200 feet, a few going as deep as 230 feet. The water is cold and murky—"like iced coffee," one diver muttered through trembling lips. Currents run to 2 knots. Visibility is often less than 10 feet. Blue sharks cruise around divers. Cables and wires tangle the ship's superstructure. If one thing can be said about salvage diving on the *Andrea Doria,* it's that it is a challenge.

CAREERS IN COMMERCIAL DIVING

For the serious person who is interested in making his sport a profession, commercial diving can open a whole new way of life. Most commercial divers serve the offshore oil industry, working on drilling rigs in all parts of the world. It is a tough occupation, but for a sharp, well-trained professional it can be quite lucrative.

Becoming a commercial diver requires more than enthusiasm and skill as a sport diver. A commercial diver must know what needs to be done and be capable of doing it in the shortest possible time, and this means mastery of hard-hat diving, semiclosed scuba, saturation diving, underwater welding, communications systems, and many other advanced technical skills. On-the-job training is the only way to gain the experience needed for such rigorous work, once the basics have been learned at a good commercial diving school. Most schools are located in coastal cities and are listed in the telephone directory.

Appendix A

Notes on Decompression and Repetitive Diving

The following notes sum up what you should know about diving beyond the no-decompression limits, as discussed in Chapter 4. Familiarize yourself with these rules and remember them.

DECOMPRESSION SICKNESS

1. All scuba divers should know the cause, symptoms, treatment, and prevention of decompression sickness. They should have available the telephone number, location, and method of transportation to the nearest decompression chamber. Call ahead to the chamber to be sure it is operational.

2. Factors which increase the likelihood of decompression sickness are extreme water temperatures, dehydration, age, obesity, poor physical condition, fatigue, alcoholic indulgence, old injuries which cause poor circulation, and heavy work during the dive.

3. The most frequent errors related to the treatment of decompression sickness are failures to do the following: to report symptoms or signs early, to treat doubtful cases, to treat promptly, to treat adequately, to recognize serious symptoms, and to keep the patient near the chamber after treatment.

DECOMPRESSION TABLES

4. A "no-decompression dive" is a dive which requires no decompression stops; however, nitrogen still goes into solution within the body. This nitrogen must be taken into account as residual nitrogen in repetitive diving. The ascent rate of 60 feet per minute is a form of decompression.

5. Bottom time starts when the diver leaves the surface and ends only when the diver starts a direct ascent back to the surface.

6. If a dive was particularly cold or arduous, or the depth/time determination may be inaccurate, or some factor increases the likelihood of decompression sickness, decompress for the next deeper and longer dive.

7. Do not fly for 12 hours after diving. After a decompression dive do not fly for 24 hours.

8. An exception to the tables occurs when a repetitive dive is to the same or greater depth than the previous dive and the surface interval is short enough that the residual nitrogen time is greater than the actual bottom time of the

previous dive. In this case, add the actual bottom time of the previous dive to the actual bottom time of the repetitive dive and decompress for the total bottom time and deepest dive.

9. Plan repetitive dives so that each successive dive is to a lesser depth. This will aid in the elimination of nitrogen and decrease the need for decompression stops. Always keep surface intervals as long as possible.

10. Plan your dive and dive your plan, always having an alternate plan if the actual depth and/or time of the dive is greater than planned.

REASONS FOR REPETITIVE DIVE PLANNING

11. To avoid decompression stops: (a) be able to use tables to compute the maximum time of a repetitive dive without decompression stops and (b) be able to use tables to compute the minimum surface interval needed to avoid decompression stops.

12. To stay within a particular decompression schedule or repetitive group.

13. To dive the maximum depth or time on limited air.

14. To make a minimum of decompression stops.

15. To make the dive and take whatever decompression stops are required.

HIGH-ALTITUDE DIVING

High-altitude diving is a special form of diving, and corrections to the dive tables and to your depth gauge must be made. You must seek out proper procedures and instruction from a diving instructor well versed in high-altitude, freshwater diving in dives in excess of 1000 feet elevation.

Divers Alert Network is recognized by almost every American diving organization as a valuable safety and educational network.

Appendix B
Dive Tables

The material that follows and the information for the use of the NAUI tables are taken from the U.S. Navy Diving Manual. Although that manual was not originally designed for the sport diver, its tables remain the most widely accepted. Even so, several new forms of dive tables are being developed, including a revision of the U.S. Navy tables. Such tables are one of the simplest forms for establishing a complete diving scenario.

When air is breathed under pressure, the inert nitrogen diffuses into the various tissues of the body. Nitrogen uptake by the body continues at different rates for the various tissues as long as the partial pressure of the inspired nitrogen is higher than the partial pressure of the gas absorbed in the tissues. Consequently, the amount of nitrogen absorbed increases with the partial pressure of the inspired nitrogen (depth) and the duration of the exposure (time).

When the diver begins to ascend, the process is reversed as the nitrogen partial pressure in the tissues exceeds that in the circulatory and respiratory systems. The pressure gradient from the tissues to the blood and lungs must be carefully controlled to prevent too rapid a diffusion of nitrogen. If the pressure gradient is uncontrolled, bubbles of nitrogen gas can form in tissues and blood, which results in the development of decompression sickness.

To prevent the development of decompression sickness, special decompression tables have been established. These tables take into consideration the amount of nitrogen absorbed by the body at various depths for given time periods. They also consider allowable pressure gradients which can exist without excessive bubble formation, and the different gas elimination rates associated with various body tissues.

Stage decompression, requiring stops of specific durations at given depths, is used for air diving because of its operational simplicity. It will be found that the decompression tables require longer stops at more frequent intervals as the surface is approached because of the higher gas expansion ratios which occur at shallow depths.

The USN decompression tables are the result of years of scientific study, calculation, animal and human experimentation, and extensive field experience. They represent the best overall information available and must be rigidly followed to ensure maximum diving safety.

The tables present a series of decompression schedules which must be followed during an ascent following an air dive. Each decompression table has specific conditions which justify its selection. These conditions are basically depth and duration of the dive to be conducted, availability of a recompression chamber, and specific environmental conditions such as sea state, water temperature, etc.

Terms frequently used in discussions of the decompression tables are defined as follows:

Depth: When used to indicate the depth of a dive, means the maximum depth attained during the dive, measured in feet of seawater.

Bottom Time: The total elapsed time from when the diver leaves the surface in descent to the time (next whole minute) that he begins his ascent, measured in minutes.

Decompression Stop: Specified depth at which a diver must remain for a specified length of time to eliminate inert gases from his body.

Single Dive: Any dive conducted after twelve hours of a previous dive.

Residual Nitrogen: Nitrogen gas that is still dissolved in a diver's tissues after he has surfaced.

Surface Interval Time (SIT): The time which a diver has spent on the surface following a dive, beginning as soon as the diver surfaces and ending as soon as he starts his next descent.

Repetitive Dive: Any dive conducted within a twelve-hour period of a previous dive.

Repetitive Group Designation: A letter which relates directly to the amount of residual nitrogen in a diver's body for a twelve-hour period following a dive.

Residual Nitrogen Time (RNT): An amount of time, in minutes, which must be added to the bottom time of a repetitive dive to compensate for the nitrogen still in solution in a diver's tissues from a previous dive.

Adjusted No-Decompression Limits (ANDL): Actual bottom time should not exceed this number.

SELECTION OF DECOMPRESSION SCHEDULE

The decompression schedules of all the tables are given in 10- or 20-foot depth increments and, usually, ten-minute bottom time increments. Depth and bottom time combinations from actual dives, however, rarely exactly match one of the decompression schedules listed in the table being used. As assurance that the selected decompression schedule is always conservative: (1) Always select the schedule depth to be equal to or the next depth greater than the actual depth to which the dive was conducted. (2) Always select the schedule bottom time to be equal to or the next longer bottom time than the actual bottom time of the dive.

For example, if the Standard Air Decompression Table was being used to select the correct schedule for a dive to 97 feet for 31 minutes, decompression would be carried out in accordance with the 100/40 schedule. NEVER ATTEMPT TO INTERPOLATE BETWEEN DECOMPRESSION SCHEDULES.

If the diver was exceptionally cold during the dive, or if his work load was relatively strenuous, the next longer decompression schedule than the one he would normally follow should be selected. For example, the normal schedule for a dive to 90 feet for 34 minutes would be the 90/40 schedule. If the diver were exceptionally cold or fatigued, he should decompress according to the 90/50 schedule.

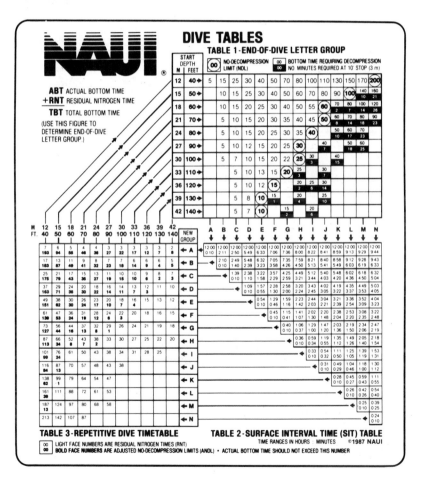

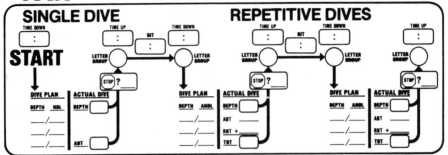

TERMS AND ABBREVIATIONS USED IN DIVE PLANNING

Single Dive–Any dive made *more than* 12 hours after a previous dive.

Repetitive Dive–Any dive made *less than* 12 hours after a previous dive.

Depth–The deepest point reached during any part of the dive.

ABT–Actual Bottom Time. On any dive, the time actually spent underwater. (This differs from the U.S. Navy's definition.)

NDL–No-Decompression Limit. On *Single Dives*, the maximum amount of Actual Bottom Time (ABT) you can spend at a particular depth, and still return to the surface without decompressing.

Letter Group–A letter symbol for the amount of *Residual Nitrogen* left in your system from previous dives.

SIT–Surface Interval Time. The time spent *sitting* on the surface between dives.

RNT–Residual Nitrogen Time. On *Repetitive Dives*, the amount of time you need to consider you've *already spent underwater* at the *start* of the dive, based on residual nitrogen left in your system from previous dives.

ANDL–Adjusted No-Decompression Limit. On *Repetitive Dives*, the maximum amount of Actual Bottom Time (ABT) you can spend at a particular depth, and still return to the surface without decompressing.

TBT–Total Bottom Time. The sum of Actual Bottom Time (ABT) and Residual Nitrogen Time (RNT). *Following Repetitive Dives*, use this figure to determine your End-of-Dive Letter Group.

©1987 NAUI

── REMEMBER ──
- Consider all dives made *shallower* than *40'* as 40' dives (12 m).
- On *any* dive, ascend no faster than 1 foot (1/3 m) per second.
- Always allow *at least 10 minutes* on the surface between dives.
- For maximum bottom times, make all Repetitive Dives to the same depth or shallower than your previous dive.

RULES DURING ASCENT

After the correct decompression schedule has been selected, it is imperative that it be exactly followed. Without exception, decompression must be completed according to the selected schedule.

Ascend at a rate of 60 feet per minute when using all tables, and locate the chest as close as possible to the stop depth.

The decompression stop times, as specified in each decompression schedule, begin as soon as the diver reaches the stop depth. Upon completion of the specified stop time, the diver ascends to the next stop, or to the surface, at the proper ascent rate. DO NOT INCLUDE ASCENT TIME AS PART OF STOP TIME.